Mindful Match

Finding Love Without Losing Yourself

by

Andres Ramirez Martinez

Table of Contents

Foreword

Embarking on a quest for love and fulfillment in a relationship often involves more than mere luck or chance—it's a profound journey of self- discovery and personal growth. This book is not merely a guide to finding love; it's an odyssey towards understanding oneself, forging a path toward deep, meaningful connections once that self-awareness is established. In these pages, we delve into the essence of building a healthy foundation within ourselves first, setting the stage for relationships that are not just surviving but thriving.

The importance of self-care and mental health in the context of relationships cannot be overstated. It is akin to the oxygen mask principle on airplanes—you must secure your mask before helping others. Similarly, nourishing your mental health and practicing self-care are critical steps in ensuring you can engage in healthy, fulfilling relationships. It's not just about being the best you can be for someone else, but about being the best version of yourself, for yourself. This personal development journey empowers you to approach dating with confidence, resilience, and a clear sense of what you seek in a partner.

Our exploration begins with a simple yet often overlooked premise: understanding and loving yourself sets a precedent for the relationships you form. Through the chapters of this book, you'll be guided through the intricacies of self-discovery, understanding your past patterns, and envisioning your future dreams. It's about acknowledging where you've been and where you'd like to go, and how the relationship with yourself is the cornerstone of any relationship you'll have with others.

As we delve deeper, we'll explore the facets of emotional independence, crafting a fulfilling single life, and cultivating emotional resilience. These principles stand as the bedrock upon which healthy relationships are built. By fostering a strong, independent sense of self, you become more capable of forming partnerships that are balanced, equal, and deeply satisfying. The journey through these pages aims to equip you with the insights and tools necessary to navigate not just the dating world but to cherish and maintain the loving relationships you forge.

The path to love and fulfillment in relationships is multifaceted, requiring a deep commitment to self-growth and mindfulness. This book endeavors to be your compass, guiding you through the valleys and peaks of dating and relationships with wisdom, empathy, and a profound understanding of the human heart. As you turn these pages, remember that the journey of a thousand miles begins with a single step—a step towards understanding, embracing, and loving yourself fully.

A Note from a Mental Health Professional on the Importance of Self-Care in Relationships

In the grand tapestry of relationships, where emotions weave in and out in complex patterns, the thread of self-care often seems to get lost. It's something that feels counterintuitive to many, with common misconceptions pinning self-care as a selfish act. However, embracing self-care is far from self-indulgent; it is essential for cultivating healthy, sustainable relationships. Like a plant needs water to thrive, individuals need self-care to nurture their emotional, mental, and physical wellbeing. When we're in a healthy state of mind, we can connect more authentically, empathize more deeply, and love more freely.

Self-care in relationships acts as a beacon, guiding us back to our center when the waters get rough. It's not just about spa days or solo vacations; it's found in the nuanced moments of everyday life. Setting boundaries, for instance, is a powerful form of self-care. Saying 'no' when we need to, allowing ourselves to be vulnerable in safe spaces, and even engaging in hobbies and interests outside of our relationships help maintain our sense of self. These practices ensure that we do not lose ourselves in the process of loving another. They also mitigate the risk of codependency, fostering a relationship dynamic where both parties maintain their individuality while being part of a healthy union.

Moreover, self-care empowers us to handle conflicts with grace and compassion. It is the bedrock upon which resilience is built, enabling us to navigate the inevitable challenges that arise within relationships with a clear mind and a grounded heart. When we take the time to care for ourselves, we're better equipped to support our partner through their struggles and share in their triumphs genuinely. So, while the journey towards love might seem daunting at first, integrating self-care into the fabric of our relationships can illuminate the path to a fulfilling and enduring partnership.

****

In this journey that we're about to embark on together, it's essential to start by looking inward, fostering self-awareness, and fortifying our mental and emotional well-being. The essence of pursuing love and establishing deep, meaningful connections with others begins with the relationship we hold with ourselves. It's easy to get lost in the pursuit of companionship or drown in the nuances of dating. Yet, understanding the core of who we are, what we need, and how we function independently sets the stage for inviting love that complements and enriches our life. This book aims to guide you through a reflective and enlightening path—starting with self-discovery, transitioning into the dating world with a sturdy foundation, and eventually, cultivating thriving, healthy relationships. The emphasis here is on mental health as a pivotal aspect of navigating these stages with grace, resilience, and a deep sense of self-worth. Let's begin this expedition together, with open hearts and minds, ready to explore the multifaceted layers of love, dating, and personal growth.

The Journey to Love: Why Mental Health Matters

Embarking on the quest for love is not just a matter of the heart; it's deeply intertwined with the complexities of our minds. Mental health plays a pivotal role in every step of this journey, from the first flutter of attraction to the deep, enduring connections we yearn for. It's the foundation upon which we build our understanding of ourselves, our desires, and our capacity to engage in healthy, fulfilling relationships. Acknowledging its importance is the first step in navigating the intricate dance of love with grace and resilience.

When we talk about mental health in the context of finding and maintaining love, we're not just referring to the absence of mental illness. It's about possessing a level of emotional and psychological wellbeing that allows us to approach relationships with openness, honesty, and vulnerability. A healthy mental state enables us to recognize and communicate our needs, set and respect boundaries, and engage in effective conflict resolution. Moreover, it allows us to appreciate our worth, ensuring we don't settle for relationships that diminish our spirits.

However, the journey to achieving and maintaining this state of wellbeing is not always smooth. The pressures of societal expectations, past traumas, and the fear of rejection can all take a toll on our mental health. It's crucial, then, to cultivate practices that bolster our emotional resilience. Whether it's through therapy, mindfulness, or self-care rituals, investing in our mental health is investing in our capacity to love and be loved. It's about building a resilient core that can weather the storms of doubt, insecurity, and conflict that invariably accompany intimate relationships.

This emphasis on mental health is not meant to discourage but to empower. It's a reminder that the strength of our relationships is a reflection of the health of our minds. By fostering a compassionate, understanding relationship with ourselves, we lay the groundwork for building connections with others that are rooted in mutual respect, empathy, and genuine affection. It transforms the quest for love from a search for completion by another to a journey of mutual growth and deepening companionship.

As we delve deeper into the subsequent chapters, we'll explore the various aspects of knowing ourselves, managing our emotions, and engaging with potential partners in a way that honors our mental wellbeing. Remember, the journey to love is as much about discovering who we are and nurturing our mental health as it is about finding that special someone. When we approach it from a place of emotional strength and clarity, we're not just better lovers — we're better, more fulfilled individuals.

Chapter 1

Self-Discovering Before Seeking

Embarking on a journey toward love and intimacy begins long before we ever swipe right on a dating app or exchange glances across a crowded room. It starts within the quiet recesses of our own minds and hearts, in the often unnoticed moments when we're truly alone with our thoughts, dreams, and insecurities. This chapter delves into the crucial first step on this journey: self-discovery. Before we can seek to understand and be understood by another, we must first turn our gaze inward, exploring the vast landscapes of our own selves.

Self-discovery is not a destination; it's an ongoing process, much like maintaining a garden. Just as a garden thrives with regular care, so too does our understanding of ourselves. It's about asking ourselves the hard questions and being open to the sometimes uncomfortable answers. What makes us feel alive? What personal values do we hold dear? Understanding these facets of ourselves sets a strong foundation for healthy future relationships.

It's easy to believe that entering a relationship will fill voids or heal wounds we carry. This notion, while comforting, often leads to dependency and disappointment. Without realizing it, we might seek out partners who we think can 'complete' us, not understanding that completeness cannot be found in another. It comes from within, from a well of self-understanding and acceptance that we must dig for ourselves.

This journey into self-discovery also involves peeling back the layers of our past. It's about understanding our reactions, our fears, and why we love the way we do. Sometimes, it involves confronting painful memories or acknowledging parts of ourselves that we've long ignored. It's in these reflections that we begin to understand our emotional needs and how they shape our relationships.

Imagine starting a relationship like building a house. If you start with a shaky foundation, anything built upon it risks collapse. Your sense of self is that foundation. Strength, resilience, and clarity about who you are and what you want become the solid ground upon which a healthy relationship can be built.

Many skip this foundational step, rushing into relationships fueled by societal pressures or personal fears of loneliness. However, taking the time for self-discovery can transform not only how you approach dating but also the quality of connections you form. It's about shifting the focus from finding the "right" person to becoming the right person — for yourself first and foremost.

It might seem counterintuitive, but the more you know and love yourself, the more you have to offer in a relationship. You become more capable of giving love that is pure and not tainted by desperation or a need for validation. Similarly, you become better at receiving love, recognizing when it is genuine and when it is not.

Some view this inward journey as a delay or detour on the path to finding love. But it's actually the most direct route. By understanding ourselves, we set the parameters for what we want and need in a partnership. We can more easily identify potential partners who align with our values and life goals, and we're quicker to recognize when something isn't right for us.

The importance of self-esteem in this process cannot be overstated. It's the armor that protects us from settling for less than we deserve and the lens that helps us see our worth clearly. Building this self-esteem is a critical aspect of self-discovery, requiring both reflection and action. We build it by setting challenges for ourselves, by celebrating our achievements, and by learning to treat ourselves with the same compassion and respect we seek in a partner.

Although self-discovery is deeply personal, it doesn't have to be a solitary journey. Seeking support from friends, family, or a mental health professional can offer new perspectives and encouragement. Sometimes, hearing someone else describe their view of us can open our eyes to qualities we've never appreciated in ourselves.

Another aspect of self-discovery involves recognizing our own patterns in relationships. Are we repeating the same mistakes? Do we cling to certain types of partners, even when we know they're not good for us? These patterns can be illuminating, pointing us toward the unresolved issues we need to address within ourselves.

Setting goals for a healthy future partnership is a hopeful and practical outcome of self-discovery. It's not about creating a checklist for the perfect partner but rather understanding the kind of relationship dynamics that will support your growth and happiness. What does a healthy partnership look like to you? What boundaries are necessary to maintain your well-being? Answers to these questions become clearer as you become more attuned to your own needs and desires.

Inevitably, this path of self-discovery will have its challenges. There will be moments of self-doubt, of loneliness, and of frustration. But these are not signs of failure; they're part of the process. They're indicators that you're moving closer to your core, to the true essence of who you are. And it's from this core that you'll one day build a relationship that's not just about seeking love, but about sharing the abundant love you've cultivated within yourself.

So, before diving into the world of dating and seeking that connection with another, take a moment to connect with yourself. Explore your depths, confront your shadows, and celebrate your light. The journey of self-discovery before seeking is, perhaps, the most important journey you'll ever undertake, setting the stage for every relationship that follows. Let this exploration be your first step toward love—not just love for another, but a profound, enduring love for yourself.

Chapter 2

Understanding Yourself

Embarking on a journey of self-discovery is often an illuminative part of our growth, yet many of us skip this crucial step when seeking connections with others. The essence of understanding oneself cannot be overstressed, especially when it pertains to cultivating healthy relationships. It's not just about knowing your favorite color or if you prefer coffee over tea; it's delving into the deeper aspects of your personality, emotional needs, and how these dictate your interactions with others. This foundation, built on self-awareness, becomes the bedrock of all future relationships.

Exploring your personality is the first chapter in this journey. It's fascinating to unearth parts of ourselves that we've pushed aside or perhaps never even knew existed. Are you an introvert who thrives in quiet spaces, or an extrovert energized by bustling environments? How do you handle stress, conflict, and communication? Insights into these questions give you a firmer grasp of who you are and how you naturally navigate the world. Recognizing and embracing your unique traits pave the way for healthier interactions with others who can appreciate and complement your authentic self.

Next, identifying your emotional needs is akin to uncovering a treasure trove of insights about your desires in relationships. We all have these needs, whether it's the need for validation, independence, affection, or understanding. Acknowledging what you need most from a partner is a monumental step toward avoiding relationships that feel unfulfilling or drain your emotional energy. It's crucial to remember that understanding and communicating your emotional needs is not a sign of weakness but a demonstration of strength and self-respect.

The importance of self-esteem in this equation cannot be overstated. A healthy level of self-esteem acts as a shield, protecting us from settling for less than we deserve and enabling us to walk away from relationships that don't serve our best interests. It's that inner voice that reminds us of our worth, encourages us to set boundaries and pursue relationships that are nourishing and growth-oriented. Cultivating a strong sense of self-esteem is a continuous process, one that involves challenging negative self-talk, celebrating your achievements, and treating yourself with kindness and compassion.

In summary, understanding yourself is not a one-time task but an ongoing process that evolves as you grow and change. It's about being curious, open, and compassionate with yourself, peeling back the layers to reveal your core. Armed with this self-knowledge, you're better equipped to make choices that align with your true needs, values, and desires. This chapter sets the stage for the next, where we'll delve into learning from past patterns and setting goals for a healthy future partnership. As you move forward, remember that this journey of self-discovery is both rewarding and essential in building relationships that are deep, meaningful, and truly fulfilling.

Exploring Your Personality

Moving forward from the foundational aspects covered earlier, it's crucial now to divert our focus inward, to a self-exploratory journey aimed at understanding the core of who we are. Recognizing and acknowledging the multifaceted nature of our personalities isn't just about labeling ourselves with broad traits like "introverted" or "extroverted"; it's about peeling back the layers to discover the nuanced aspects of our individuality. This intricate process is both enlightening and essential for anyone preparing to navigate the realm of relationships with confidence and self-awareness.

At first glance, diving into the depths of your personality might sound like a solitary quest meant for introspective evenings. However, it's actually an engaging ongoing process that benefits greatly from interaction with the world around us. Each experience, whether it be a challenging project at work or a spontaneous road trip with friends, serves as a mirror reflecting parts of our character we may not have recognized before. It's these moments, when viewed through a lens of curiosity rather than judgment, that can reveal the most about what makes us tick, what triggers our frustrations, and what sparks joy in our hearts.

Understanding your personality isn't a static, one-time task but rather, a dynamic pursuit that evolves along with you. As you grow and adapt to new experiences, relationships, and challenges, your perceptions of yourself might shift. This is perfectly normal and reflects the complex, changing nature of human beings. Embracing this fluidity is key to fostering a strong sense of self that is resilient yet adaptable, capable of thriving in the uncertainties of life and love.

But where to start? A practical approach involves mindfulness and reflection practices that allow you to observe your feelings, thoughts, and reactions in different situations. Keeping a journal or using personality assessment tools can be helpful, but remember, these methods merely serve as guides, not definitive answers. The true essence of your personality is discovered in the day-to-day, in the decisions you make, the passions you pursue, and the way you interact with others. It's in these lived experiences that your true self shines through, offering the most authentic insights into who you are.

As we proceed to the next sections, focusing on identifying your emotional needs and the importance of self-esteem, keep in mind that the journey you've embarked upon in exploring your personality is foundational. It paves the way for a deeper understanding and appreciation of your unique self, which is invaluable not just in the realm of dating but in all aspects of life. With this self-knowledge, you'll be better equipped to establish and nurture meaningful, healthy relationships that align with your true self.

Identifying Your Emotional Needs

As we turn the page from exploring our personality to identifying our emotional needs, it's important to recognize that understanding these needs is a cornerstone of building not just any relationship, but the right one for us. Just as a plant needs sunlight, water, and soil to thrive, our emotional selves require nurturing in specific ways. By identifying what it is we truly seek emotionally, we embark on a path that leads towards more fulfilling relationships.

Firstly, let's define what emotional needs are. They can be considered as necessary components for our mental and emotional well-being — aspects such as feeling appreciated, loved, secure, and understood. Different individuals prioritize these needs differently, and there's no one-size-fits-all. It's about what makes you feel whole and supported.

To start understanding your emotional needs, introspection is key. It's about digging deep and asking yourself what makes you feel loved and valued. This might be promptness and reliability, indicating that you highly value security and stability in a relationship. Or, perhaps you find that being listened to attentively makes you feel most loved, suggesting a need for understanding and validation. Recognizing these needs is the first step towards communicating them effectively.

Why is it crucial to identify and communicate these needs? Unmet emotional needs can lead to feelings of dissatisfaction and disconnection in relationships. Imagine trying to fit a square peg into a round hole; without addressing our core needs, we might find ourselves repeatedly in relationships that feel lacking, despite not quite knowing why.

It's also essential to recognize that our emotional needs can evolve over time. What we required from a relationship in our twenties might look different in our thirties, forties, and beyond. Life experiences, personal growth, and changing circumstances all play a role in shaping these needs. Therefore, regular check-ins with yourself are recommended. It's just like updating an app on your phone; as you grow and change, so should your understanding of what you need emotionally.

Moreover, understanding our emotional needs leads to healthier boundaries. When we know what we need, we're better equipped to say 'yes' to what nourishes our hearts and 'no' to what doesn't. It enables us to steer clear of potential relationships that do not align with our needs or might detract from our well-being.

Another aspect to consider is the balance of emotional needs within a relationship. It's not just about what we need, but also what we can give. Relationships thrive on reciprocity; a mutual exchange of meeting emotional needs creates a foundation of support and understanding. It's about finding that harmony where both partners feel their needs are acknowledged and valued.

Practical steps to identify your emotional needs include journaling about times you've felt most happy and fulfilled in relationships, as well as those moments you've felt let down or neglected. Patterns will begin to emerge that can guide you towards understanding your needs better.

Additionally, engaging in open, vulnerable conversations with trusted friends or a therapist can provide insights and different perspectives.

Ultimately, knowing your emotional needs is not just a tool for building romantic relationships; it's about enhancing your relationship with yourself. It empowers you to seek out and cultivate connections that uplift and support you, both now and in the future. Plus, it sets the stage for developing a nuanced understanding of others' needs, enriching your capacity for empathy and connection.

As we move towards building self-esteem, remember that identifying your emotional needs is an ongoing process. It requires patience, honesty, and sometimes, the courage to face aspects of ourselves we've overlooked. But the reward — deeper, more meaningful connections — is well worth the journey.

The Importance of Self-Esteem

As we navigate through the complexities of understanding ourselves, it becomes evident that the bedrock of our personal development and the quality of our relationships is, without a doubt, rooted in self-esteem. This section delves into why cultivating a healthy sense of self-worth is crucial not just for individual contentment, but also as a foundational aspect of entering and sustaining fulfilling relationships.

Self-esteem influences our decisions, interactions, and our resilience in the face of challenges. When you possess a solid sense of self-esteem, you're more likely to pursue opportunities that align with your values and interests, rather than settling for less than you deserve. This inherent belief in one's value is instrumental in setting the stage for the type of relationships you form. Essentially, it acts as a filter that helps distinguish healthy, supportive partnerships from those that may be detrimental to your well-being.

It's important to recognize that self-esteem doesn't translate to an inflated ego or arrogance. Rather, it's about acknowledging your intrinsic worth, embracing your strengths and weaknesses, and treating yourself with compassion and respect. This balanced self-perception empowers you to accept love and respect from others because you believe you rightly deserve it.

How, then, does one go about building or reinforcing this critical pillar of self-esteem? It begins with a journey inward, reflecting on your thoughts, emotions, and behaviors. Notice how you talk to yourself in your moments of success and, more importantly, in your failures. Cultivating a nurturing inner voice is a vital step towards fostering a resilient sense of self-esteem.

Setting achievable goals and celebrating your accomplishments, no matter how small, can also significantly boost your self-worth. Every step forward is a testament to your abilities and perseverance, reinforcing your belief in yourself. Furthermore, surrounding yourself with people who uplift you can magnify the positive effects on your self-esteem. The company you keep can either serve to elevate your sense of self-worth or deplete it, making it essential to choose your social circles wisely.

Additionally, practicing self-compassion is a cornerstone of building self-esteem. It involves treating yourself with the same kindness and understanding you would offer a good friend. This approach helps mitigate self-criticism and fosters a more supportive relationship with yourself, which is fundamental when navigating the dating world or maintaining relationships.

On the flip side, low self-esteem can manifest in a myriad of ways that hinder personal growth and relationship satisfaction. It might lead to settling for less, tolerating unhealthy behaviors, or struggling to voice one's needs and boundaries. Recognizing these patterns is the first step towards change, signifying the need to bolster one's self-esteem as part of their journey towards healthier, more fulfilling relationships.

The implications of self-esteem extend beyond the realm of personal development. In the context of relationships, a healthy sense of self-worth enables clearer communication, the establishment and respect of boundaries, and a more balanced dynamic between partners. It's a crucial element in the foundation of any relationship that aspires to be nurturing, supportive, and lasting.

In conclusion, self-esteem is not just a nice-to-have; it's an essential aspect of who we are and how we interact with the world around us. It shapes our choices, influences our relationships, and plays a critical role in our pursuit of happiness. By investing in our self-esteem, we set the stage for a life filled with more meaningful connections, resilience in the face of adversity, and a deep, abiding sense of self-respect. As we continue this journey of self-discovery and relationship-building, let the cultivation of a healthy self-esteem be a beacon guiding us towards fulfilling and loving partnerships.

Remember, the relationship you have with yourself sets the tone for every other relationship in your life. Nurturing your self-esteem is not just a journey of self-improvement; it's a profound act of self-love that echoes through every aspect of your being and every interaction you have. As you move forward, let your newfound understanding of the importance of self-esteem be the light that guides you toward healthier, happier relationships.

Chapter 3

Past Patterns and Future Dreams

As we transition from a deep dive into understanding oneself in the previous chapters to looking ahead, "Past Patterns and Future Dreams" serves as a pivotal moment in our journey. This chapter illuminates the intricate dance between reflecting on our dating history and envisioning a future filled with healthy, fulfilling partnerships. We often carry the emotional baggage of past relationships without even realizing it, harboring patterns that may not serve our best interests. Here, we tackle these past experiences head-on, not to dwell on them but to learn from them. We analyze what has worked, what hasn't, and more importantly, why. It's about acknowledging our past to make peace with it and not letting it dictate our future relational dynamics.

But this chapter isn't just about looking backward; it's equally about setting our sights on the horizon. We transition into dreaming big about the future, but not in a whimsical, unfocused manner. We set tangible, achievable goals for what a healthy future partnership looks like. It's about crafting a vision that's both inspired and informed by our past learnings, ensuring we're not just passively hoping for a better future but actively steering ourselves towards it. This chapter is the bridge between where you've been and where you're going, providing you with the tools to navigate from one to the other with wisdom, grace, and optimism.

Learning from Past Relationships

As we embark on the crucial journey of understanding the role past relationships play in our lives, it's essential to recognize how these experiences shape our approach to future partnerships. Often, our past liaisons serve as a mirror, reflecting back the patterns and behaviors that either propel us forward or hold us back. Taking a moment to delve into these reflections isn't about assigning blame or dwelling in regret; rather, it's a powerful step towards self-awareness and growth. By identifying what worked and what didn't, we can start to unravel the complex tapestry of our emotional landscape.

One common thread many of us find when looking back is a tendency to repeat certain patterns, whether it's the type of partner we choose, how we communicate in times of conflict, or the way we prioritize our needs versus those of our partner. It's easy to fall into familiar behaviors, even when they don't serve our best interests. However, bringing these patterns to light isn't an exercise in futility. On the contrary, recognizing and understanding these patterns is the first step in choosing not to repeat them. This process involves introspection and, occasionally, some uncomfortable truths about our role in these dynamics. But with this awareness comes the power to instigate change.

Learning from our past also means acknowledging the growth that each relationship has fostered within us. Every partnership, no matter how it ended, offered lessons and opportunities for personal development. Perhaps it taught you more about your emotional needs, or it might have highlighted the importance of communication and transparency in a relationship. Whatever the takeaway, these lessons are invaluable. They equip us with knowledge and insight, making us better partners in future relationships. It's akin to collecting pieces of a puzzle; each piece is essential in completing the bigger picture of who we are and what we seek in a partner.

Moreover, this journey of reflection and learning isn't meant to be undertaken alone. Engaging in open dialogues with trusted friends, family, or even a therapist can provide new perspectives and insights. Sometimes, an outside view can highlight aspects we may overlook or underestimate in our self-assessment. This external input can be incredibly validating and enlightening, helping to reinforce our discoveries and encourage our progress. It's a reminder that while the exploration of past relationships is a personal journey, you don't have to navigate it in isolation.

In sum, the path to understanding and learning from our past relationships is both challenging and immensely rewarding. It requires honesty, vulnerability, and a willingness to confront our shortcomings. Yet, the knowledge and self-awareness gained through this process are indispensable. They lay the foundation for healthier, more fulfilling relationships in the future, allowing us to approach love with heightened awareness, compassion, and resilience. By learning from the past, we're not just moving on; we're moving forward, equipped with the insights and wisdom to create the loving, supportive partnerships we desire and deserve.

Setting Goals for a Healthy Future Partnership

Turning the page on past relationships and focusing on the future requires intention and clarity, especially when dreaming of a healthy, meaningful partnership. It's about striking a balance between learning from past experiences and not letting them define or limit your future happiness. Setting goals for your future relationship is not just wishful thinking; it's creating a roadmap for your heart and mind.

First and foremost, consider what emotional needs are most important to you in a relationship. Is it understanding, respect, or perhaps unwavering support? Recognizing these needs can help you visualize the kind of partnership that will not only bring you joy but also nurture your growth. It's vital to remember that while no relationship is perfect, setting your sights on a partnership that aligns with your core emotional needs is a step in the right direction.

Reflecting on past patterns is invaluable in this process. Consider the lessons learned from previous relationships and how they can inform your future choices. This reflection isn't about dwelling on the past but about recognizing patterns that may have hindered your happiness. By doing so, you're better equipped to make conscious choices that support a healthier relationship dynamic moving forward.

Effective communication stands at the heart of any healthy relationship. Setting a goal to develop and maintain open, honest, and respectful communication is crucial. This means not only sharing your thoughts and feelings but also actively listening to your partner's perspectives. Cultivating this kind of communication can build a strong foundation for mutual understanding and respect.

Another essential goal is to maintain your individuality within the partnership. It's easy to lose oneself in the whirlwind of romance, but a healthy relationship promotes personal growth alongside the growth of the relationship. Encourage each other's personal interests and goals, recognizing that individuality adds depth and strength to the partnership.

Trust and vulnerability go hand in hand as foundational elements of a secure relationship. Aiming to build trust gradually, showing patience and reliability, can foster a safe space for both partners to share their vulnerabilities without fear of judgment. This level of emotional intimacy is where deep connections are nurtured.

Boundaries are equally important in picturing your future relationship. Understanding and respecting each other's boundaries can prevent misunderstandings and conflicts. It's about knowing where you end and the other person begins, honoring each other's needs for personal space, and time apart, even within the closeness of a partnership.

Finally, remember that a healthy relationship is a partnership of equals, where both parties contribute to the relationship's growth and well-being. It's about teamwork, where the success and happiness of the relationship are shared goals that require effort and dedication from both individuals.

In setting these goals for a healthy future partnership, it's important to approach them with flexibility. Life is unpredictable, and relationships evolve. These goals aren't set in stone but are guideposts to keep you aligned with the kind of relationship that enriches your life. By aiming for a partnership infused with respect, understanding, and mutual growth, you're not only investing in your future happiness but also in your personal journey of growth and self-discovery.

As you move forward, let these goals light your path towards a fulfilling and healthy partnership. Remember, it's the journey that shapes us, and striving for a relationship that aligns with these ideals is a journey worth taking. So, take it one step at a time, stay true to yourself, and trust that you're moving closer to the relationship you envision and deserve.

Chapter 4

Emotional Independence

Building upon the solid foundation of self-discovery and reflection on past relationships, we pivot to a crucial aspect of personal development: emotional independence. This concept, often overlooked, is the bedrock upon which a fulfilling single life and, eventually, a healthy, resilient relationship is built. It's the ability to source happiness and contentment from within, rather than relying on others to fill that void. This chapter delves into not just the significance of emotional independence, but practical ways to cultivate and nurture it.

Emotional independence doesn't mean isolating oneself or shunning relationships. Rather, it cultivates a space where one's emotional well-being isn't heavily dependent on the validation or actions of others. This journey begins with a conscious decision to prioritize self-love and self-care. It's about developing a fulfilling single life that resonates with your innermost desires and needs. This doesn't happen overnight, and indeed, it requires consistent effort and introspection. Engaging in activities that enrich your mind, body, and spirit are foundational steps. Whether it's pursuing a long-held passion, investing in personal growth, or simply finding joy in the rhythm of daily life, these experiences reinforce the belief that your own company is not just enough, but deeply satisfying.

Cultivating emotional resilience is another cornerstone of emotional independence. Life, by its nature, is unpredictable—filled with ups and downs. Building resilience equips you to handle life's challenges without being overwhelmed and to bounce back from setbacks stronger than before. Techniques such as mindfulness meditation, journaling, and cognitive-behavioral strategies can fortify your mental and emotional robustness. Moreover, nurturing a supportive social network plays a complementary role. Having strong, positive relationships in your life—be they family, friends, or community connections—provides a safety net that fosters independence rather than co-dependence.

Importantly, emotional independence also means recognizing when to seek help. It's a sign of strength, not weakness, to ask for support when needed. Whether it's consulting a therapist, reaching out to a trusted friend, or engaging in supportive groups, acknowledging the need for external assistance is a step toward safeguarding your emotional health. This balance of self-reliance and knowing when to lean on others is a hallmark of true emotional independence.

In conclusion, emotional independence is not a destination but a continuous journey. It's a process of learning, growth, and self-renewal that enhances your capacity for joy, resilience, and fulfillment—both within yourself and in relationships with others. By building a life that's fulfilling on your own terms, you lay the groundwork for not just surviving on your own, but thriving—ready to enter or enhance a relationship from a position of strength, not necessity. Through this lens, we see that emotional independence is not just beneficial, but essential for building healthy, fulfilling relationships.

Building a Fulfilling Single Life

Emerging from the foundational understanding of oneself, it's essential to pivot towards constructing a fulfilling life as a single individual. This isn't merely a pit stop on the journey towards partnership; it's a rich, vibrant chapter of your life where immense personal growth and satisfaction can be achieved. The path to emotional independence is both challenging and rewarding, demanding a concerted effort to embrace solitude not as a void to be filled, but as a serene space for self-reflection and self-improvement.

This process begins with the recognition that happiness and fulfillment come from within. It's a common misconception to view a romantic relationship as the panacea for all of life's problems or a void-filler. However, relying on someone else for your happiness is like building a house on sand—it can shift away at any moment. The quest, then, is to find stable ground within yourself, erecting the foundations of your satisfaction and contentment on your own achievements, passions, and the rich tapestry of relationships with friends and family.

Investing in your interests and passions is not just a pastime—it's an act of self-love and a declaration of your worth. Whether it's art, music, sports, or any other activity that ignites your spirit, these endeavors provide a sense of achievement and joy that is completely within your control, unlike the unpredictable nature of romantic relationships. Furthermore, these activities can become a source of connection with like-minded individuals, enriching your social circle and providing a supportive community.

Setting personal goals outside of relationship ambitions is also crucial. Whether it's career objectives, fitness targets, or learning new skills, these goals provide a sense of purpose and direction. Achieving these can boost your self-esteem and provide tangible evidence of your capabilities, reinforcing the fact that your worth isn't contingent upon being in a relationship.

Another important aspect is cultivating self-awareness and mindfulness. Understanding your thought patterns, emotions, and reactions leads to a deeper self-appreciation and the skill to navigate life's ups and downs with grace. Mindfulness practices can help you stay present and find joy in the moment, reducing the need for external validation or companionship to feel complete.

Building a strong support network is also vital. Surrounding yourself with friends, family members, and mentors who encourage your growth and support your journey towards emotional independence not only provides a safety net during tough times but also enriches your life with meaningful connections. These relationships can offer the same depth of love, support, and fulfillment traditionally sought in romantic partnerships.

Learning to enjoy your own company is perhaps the pinnacle of building a fulfilling single life. Discovering solace, peace, and even joy in being alone is a powerful step towards emotional independence. It's the realization that your company is enough, and solitude can be a profound experience of self-discovery and self-care. It means listening to your needs, treating yourself kindly, and cherishing the quiet moments where you can truly connect with yourself.

However, embodying a fulfilling single life doesn't imply closing the door on romantic relationships. Instead, it's about approaching them from a place of abundance, not lack—a perspective where a partnership adds to your life, instead of being seen as a missing piece. This mindset shift is fundamental to entering future relationships with clarity, confidence, and the strength to maintain your identity within the partnership.

In conclusion, building a fulfilling single life is not a holding pattern until someone comes along. It's an active, dynamic process of self-improvement, self-discovery, and self-love. By embracing your single status as an opportunity rather than a shortfall, you set the stage for not just a fulfilling relationship with others, but most importantly, an enduring, loving relationship with yourself.

As you cultivate this fulfilling single life, remember, the journey toward emotional independence is unique for everyone. It's filled with its own set of challenges and triumphs. However, the effort put into this chapter of your life will not only make you a more content, resilient individual but also prepare you for a healthier, more fulfilling partnership in the future. Embrace it, cherish it, and let it unfold.

Cultivating Emotional Resilience

As we continue our journey into the heart of emotional independence, we arrive at a vital pit stop that's often overlooked: cultivating emotional resilience. Building resilience isn't just about being strong in the face of adversity; it's about developing a deep well of emotional resources to draw upon during the challenging times that inevitably crop up in our lives and relationships.

At its core, emotional resilience is the ability to bounce back from setbacks, cope with stress, and adapt to new circumstances with ease and agility. It's a skill, not an innate trait, which means it can be developed and honed over time. In the realm of emotional independence, resilience serves as our shield and compass, allowing us to navigate the complexities of relationships with greater confidence and self-assurance.

One of the first steps in cultivating emotional resilience is recognizing that setbacks and challenges are not only inevitable but also instrumental in our growth. They provide us with invaluable opportunities to learn more about ourselves, our needs, and our capacities. Viewing difficulties through this lens transforms them from insurmountable obstacles into stepping stones on our path to self-discovery and emotional independence.

Another key aspect of building resilience is developing a positive self- dialogue. The way we talk to ourselves during tough times significantly influences our ability to cope and recover. Encouraging oneself with empathy and understanding, as opposed to self-criticism, fosters resilience by reinforcing our inner strength and resourcefulness.

Self-care is another critical component of emotional resilience. Engaging in activities that nourish both the body and mind, such as exercise, meditation, and creative pursuits, equips us with a stronger emotional foundation, making us less susceptible to being overwhelmed by stressors or emotional upheavals in our lives and relationships.

Embracing vulnerability plays a crucial role in building emotional resilience. It might seem counterintuitive, but acknowledging our fears, insecurities, and uncertainties is a powerful act of courage. Vulnerability allows us to face our challenges head-on, armed with a genuine understanding of our boundaries and limitations, which is essential for personal growth and emotional independence.

Developing a network of support is instrumental in cultivating emotional resilience. Having a circle of friends, family, or professionals we trust and can turn to during challenging times provides us with a sense of belonging and community. This support system acts as a vital safety net, reminding us that we don't have to face hardships alone.

Mindfulness and living in the present moment are also significant aspects of resilience. By focusing on the here and now, rather than dwelling on past mistakes or worrying about future problems, we can reduce our stress levels and improve our emotional well-being.

Mindfulness encourages a compassionate, non-judgmental attitude towards ourselves and our experiences, facilitating a more resilient outlook on life.

Setting realistic goals and expectations is another essential strategy for fostering emotional resilience. When we set attainable objectives, we not only increase our chances of success but also reduce the likelihood of facing overwhelming disappointment. Realistic expectations help us approach challenges with a sense of purpose and direction, vital for maintaining our emotional equilibrium.

Learning to let go of what we can't control is a liberating aspect of cultivating emotional resilience. By focusing our energy on the aspects of our lives that we have the power to change, rather than fixating on uncontrollable outcomes, we foster a sense of empowerment and autonomy that bolsters our emotional independence.

Adapting to change is another crucial element of resilience. Life and relationships are in a constant state of flux, so our ability to adapt to new situations is key to navigating these changes successfully. Embracing change rather than resisting it encourages personal growth and strengthens our emotional resilience.

Practicing gratitude is a simple yet profoundly impactful way to cultivate resilience. By focusing on what we're thankful for, even during tough times, we shift our perspective from one of lack to one of abundance. Gratitude fosters positive emotions and reduces stress, making it easier to bounce back from setbacks.

In essence, cultivating emotional resilience is about nurturing a relationship with ourselves that's based on kindness, compassion, and understanding. It's about recognising our strengths and limitations and understanding that both are integral to our journey towards emotional independence.

As we build our resilience, we equip ourselves with the tools needed not only to face life's challenges but to emerge from them stronger, more self-aware, and more emotionally independent. Through resilience, we discover that we are not defined by the difficulties we encounter but by how we respond to them.

In the following sections, we will delve deeper into how these aspects of emotional resilience play a crucial role in preparing for and navigating the complexities of relationships. By fostering emotional resilience, we lay a solid foundation for healthy, fulfilling partnerships that enhance our journey towards love and self-discovery.

Chapter 5

Preparing for a Healthy Relationship

As we transition from the foundation of self-love and emotional independence, it becomes pivotal to consciously prepare ourselves for the world of healthy relationships. It's akin to setting the stage for the most significant play of our lives, where every role, every act, must be performed with intention and clarity. The groundwork laid in previous chapters serves as the bedrock upon which the ethos of a healthy relationship is built. Now, let's delve into how we can actively gear up for relationships that not only bring joy but foster growth and mutual respect.

The cornerstone of preparing for a healthy relationship is understanding that it's an extension of our well-being, not a solution to our problems or an escape from loneliness. This entails a profound appreciation for the notion that a relationship can only be as healthy as the individuals in it. Taking time to cultivate your interests, maintaining your friendships, and pursuing personal growth are not just acts of self-care; they are investments in the health of your future relationships. When two individuals, who are content and complete on their own, come together, they create a partnership that's rooted in mutual respect and genuine affection, rather than dependency or fear of solitude.

Furthermore, developing a keen sense of self-awareness and emotional intelligence plays a crucial role in preparing for a relationship. It's about knowing not just what makes you happy or sad, but understanding how you handle stress, conflict, and disagreement. Mastering the art of communication is also fundamental. The ability to express your thoughts and feelings openly and respectfully, and to listen to and truly understand your partner, is the linchpin of a healthy relationship. As such, honing these skills now, outside of a romantic context, will make them second nature when the time comes to apply them in partnership.

Another essential aspect is setting realistic expectations. Romantic comedies and fairy tales have, for too long, painted an unrealistic picture of relationships. Understanding that disagreements are normal, that no one is perfect, and that relationships require effort, compromise, and sometimes, hard work, is vital. Preparing yourself for the realities of sharing your life with another person means embracing imperfections - both yours and your partner's - with compassion and grace.

Last but certainly not least, knowing what you're looking for in a relationship and not compromising on your fundamental values and beliefs is critical. While it's important to be flexible and open-minded, staying true to your core principles and non-negotiables is essential for long-term compatibility and fulfillment. As we move forward, keeping these preparatory steps in mind will not only guide us towards healthy relationships but will also enhance our journey towards finding and maintaining them. With a strong, self-aware foundation and a clear vision of what we seek, we equip ourselves with the tools necessary to navigate the complexities of relationships with resilience and grace.

Chapter 6

Defining Healthy Relationships

As we venture further into the essence of what it truly means to nurture a healthy, sustainable partnership, it becomes paramount to outline the foundational elements that constitute such a relationship. At its core, a healthy relationship is marked by a mutual respect for one another's individuality, an enduring support system that both partners contribute to, and an open line of communication that allows for the expression of both joys and concerns. It's about understanding that while two people may walk side by side, they also maintain their separate identities and personal growth trajectories.

In the labyrinth of human connections, a positive partnership thrives on balance. This balance isn't about keeping score or ensuring everything is 50/50; rather, it's about each person contributing to the relationship in ways that feel equitable and fulfilling to both parties. Trust, a cornerstone of any deep and meaningful relationship, is built over time through consistent actions, reliability, and open, honest communication. Yet, it's also about knowing when to offer space— acknowledging that trust includes giving each other the room to be individuals with their own interests, friendships, and time for solitude.

Recognizing red flags is equally critical in defining what a healthy relationship isn't. It's about being vigilant towards behaviors that undermine the very foundation of respect, equality, and trust that a positive partnership is built on. This involves being mindful of patterns that could potentially lead to manipulation, control, or disrespect, and addressing them promptly or seeking support if necessary. Defining a healthy relationship isn't just about understanding and striving for the ideals but also being acutely aware of what it should never become. As we explore the roles of communication, boundaries, and self-care in the following chapters, keeping these fundamental principles in mind will guide us toward nurturing relationships that not only survive but thrive.

Characteristics of a Positive Partnership

Embarking on the quest for love and companionship is a rollercoaster filled with highs, lows, and everything in between. However, at the core of every heart-fluttering, soul-stirring connection lies the foundation of a positive partnership. When two individuals come together in a relationship built on mutual respect, understanding, and genuine affection, the journey becomes not just bearable but beautiful.

A significant hallmark of a strong partnership is open and honest communication. It's the ability to share your thoughts, fears, dreams, and desires without fear of judgment. It's more than just talking about how your day went. It's about feeling safe enough to express your vulnerabilities and knowing your partner is truly listening. This level of communication strengthens the bond between partners, making them feel seen, heard, and valued.

Trust is another cornerstone of a positive relationship. It's cultivated over time through consistent actions that match words, creating a secure environment where love can flourish. Trust encompasses faith in each other's commitment, the security in knowing that confidences are kept, and the belief that your partner will always have your best interest at heart. With trust, you can navigate the uncertainties of life with the confidence that you're not alone.

Respect in a partnership reflects in valuing each other's opinions, feelings, and boundaries. It means honoring the differences that make each person unique without an attempt to change them. This respect is vital for fostering individuality within the relationship, allowing each person to grow without fear of losing their essence. It's the understanding that love is not possessive but liberating, giving each partner the space to be their true self.

Empathy plays a crucial role in understanding and connecting with your partner on a deeper level. It involves putting yourself in their shoes, feeling with them, and providing comfort during tough times. An empathetic approach can diffuse conflicts and promote a deeper understanding between partners, highlighting their emotional needs and how best to support them.

Moreover, a positive partnership encourages personal growth. Instead of one partner eclipsing the other, both individuals inspire each other to pursue their interests, ambitions, and self-improvement. This mutual support system reinforces the bond between them, making the relationship a source of strength and inspiration. It's about being each other's cheerleader, celebrating victories, and offering a shoulder to lean on during defeats.

Equally important is the ability to have fun together, to enjoy each other's company, and to cherish the moments spent together. Sharing laughter, hobbies, and interests adds a layer of companionship that transcends romantic love. It's the joy found in the simplicity of a shared meal, the excitement of new adventures, or the comfort of a quiet evening at home. These moments, though seemingly insignificant, are the threads that weave the tapestry of a joyful partnership.

Commitment is the glue that holds a positive partnership together. It's not just about sticking together during the sunny days but also weathering the storms as a united front. This commitment means continuously choosing each other, even when things are less than perfect, and working together to nurture and strengthen the bond.

Lastly, mutual support in a relationship goes beyond emotional backing; it extends to supporting each other's dreams and aspirations. It's about being the wind beneath each other's wings, offering practical help, encouragement, or even making sacrifices to help the other person succeed. True partnership means being each other's biggest fan and toughest critic, all while pushing each other toward greatness.

In essence, a positive partnership is built on a foundation of trust, communication, respect, empathy, personal growth, enjoyment, commitment, and mutual support. These characteristics form the bedrock of a healthy, strong, and fulfilling relationship, guiding couples as they navigate the complexities of life together. Embracing these traits can help partners not only to love but to thrive within the partnership, creating a bond that is not only enduring but truly enriching.

Recognizing Red Flags

As we've explored the components that form a healthy relationship, it's equally critical to identify the warning signs or "red flags" that can emerge. Recognizing these early on can prevent much heartache. Just like a garden that flourishes with care but withers with neglect, relationships require nurturing and mutual respect to grow.

A common red flag is a lack of communication. If your partner consistently avoids discussing important topics or expressing their feelings, it can create a barrier between you. Communication is the bridge that connects two people, allowing them to share their worlds. Without it, you're basically living on two separate islands.

Another concerning sign is when your partner exhibits controlling behavior. This could manifest as them dictating who you can see, where you can go, or even how you should dress. It's a glaring signal that they don't respect your autonomy. A relationship should be a partnership, not a dictatorship.

Jealousy, when it transcends the bounds of normal concern, can be a potent red flag. It's natural to feel protective over one's partner, but an overbearing jealousy challenges the trust and foundation of your relationship. If they're constantly questioning your whereabouts or mistrusting your intentions without cause, it's a sign of deeper issues.

Disrespect, in any form, is unacceptable. This could be overt, such as insulting remarks or mockery, or more subtle, like constant interruptions or disregarding your opinions. Regardless of its form, disrespect chips away at the relationship's core, fostering an environment of insecurity and low self-esteem.

When actions and words don't align, it's a critical red flag. If your partner makes promises but repeatedly fails to keep them, it undermines trust. Trust is like a paper; once crumpled, it can never be perfectly smooth again. Consistency between words and actions is key to building a sturdy, reliable foundation.

Gaslighting is a particularly insidious behavior. It's when your partner manipulates situations to make you doubt your perceptions or sanity. For instance, they might deny saying something you clearly remember or make you question your feelings. It's a form of psychological control that no one should have to endure.

Lack of support for your ambitions and dreams is another significant red flag. A partner worthy of your time encourages you to grow, celebrates your successes, and supports your aspirations. If they see your achievements as threats or belittle your goals, it indicates a lack of mutual respect and support fundamental to any healthy relationship.

Isolation from friends and family is a tactic often employed in unhealthy relationships. If your partner systematically criticizes or discourages interactions with your loved ones, they're not only severing your support network but also increasing your reliance on them. This is a major control strategy, signaling deeper issues.

Constant conflict or the presence of unresolvable arguments signals a misalignment in core values or communication styles. While disagreements are natural, perpetual conflict without resolution drains the relationship, leaving little room for positive growth or mutual understanding.

If your partner is reluctant to make the relationship known or keeps significant aspects of their life hidden, it's worth questioning why. Transparency and openness are pillars of trust. A relationship thrived in secrecy undercuts these foundations, breeding insecurity and doubt.

Substance abuse and the unwillingness to seek help is a red flag that can't be ignored. While it's important to support loved ones through difficulties, there's a distinction between support and enabling harmful behavior. The substance becomes a third party in the relationship, often leading to neglect, abuse, or worse.

Finally, ignoring your gut feeling is a red flag in itself. If something feels off, it's crucial to trust your instincts. Your inner voice is informed by your emotions, experiences, and perceptions. Paying attention to it could save you from further emotional turmoil.

Understanding and recognizing these red flags is vital. Knowing when to hold on and when to let go can be tough, but it's crucial for preserving your well-being. Relationships should uplift you, not leave you constantly on edge. If the bad outweighs the good, it may be time to reevaluate.

In closing, don't forget that recognizing red flags is not about finding a perfect partner but about avoiding those who detract significantly from your happiness and growth. This chapter lays the groundwork for making informed decisions, promoting self-respect, and actively seeking out healthier, more fulfilling connections.

Chapter 7

Communication and Boundaries

As we delve into the essence of what makes relationships tick, we find ourselves at the heart of two crucial elements: communication and boundaries. It's like discovering the secret ingredients that, when mixed right, can turn a bland interaction into a rich, fulfilling connection. Think about it; mastering the art of conveying our thoughts and feelings effectively is nothing short of a superpower in any relationship. But it's not just about talking; it's about engaging in a two-way dialogue where listening becomes as significant as speaking. And here's where it gets interesting - setting boundaries is not about building walls but about drawing lines in the sand that protect and respect both parties' emotional spaces. This chapter isn't just about talking the talk but walking the walk. We're going to explore how honing our communication skills and understanding the art of setting and respecting boundaries are not just acts of love for our partners but profound acts of self-love. These practices allow us to express our needs and desires clearly while graciously accepting the other person's perspective, paving the way for a relationship marked by mutual respect and understanding.

Honing Communication Skills

In any strong, healthy relationship, communication doesn't just happen by accident. It's like a garden that needs constant tending, ample sunlight, and just the right amount of water. And just as every plant has its unique requirements, every relationship has its distinct communication needs. This section delves into the nuances of nurturing those skills, ensuring that your interactions grow from a place of understanding, respect, and warmth. Taking the time to fine-tune the way we express ourselves and listen to others sets a solid foundation for thriving relationships.

To begin, it's crucial to appreciate the impact of active listening. It's not just about hearing the words another person says but truly understanding the emotions and intentions behind them. Imagine a scenario where a partner shares something that's been bothering them. By listening actively, you're not just waiting for your turn to speak; you're empathizing, reading between the lines, and responding in a way that acknowledges their feelings. This level of attentiveness fosters a deeper connection, showing your partner they're truly seen and heard. It's a cornerstone of effective communication that transforms simple exchanges into meaningful conversations.

Equally important is the art of expressing needs and desires transparently and respectfully. Often, we hold back from saying what we need, fearing it might upset the other person. However, bottling up our feelings can lead to resentment and misunderstandings. On the other side, being overly blunt can inadvertently hurt the person we care about. The key lies in finding that sweet middle ground where honesty is tempered with compassion. Phrasing matters immensely; it's about stating your needs while being considerate of the other person's feelings and perspectives.

Navigating conflicts with grace represents another facet of honed communication skills. Disagreements are natural in any relationship, but their resolution rests heavily on how issues are communicated. Approaching conflicts with a mindset of finding a solution rather than winning an argument encourages a collaborative spirit. It's important to communicate grievances in a non-accusatory manner, focusing on how certain actions made you feel rather than assigning blame. This constructive approach not only leads to resolving issues more effectively but also strengthens the relationship by building trust and understanding.

Lastly, regular, open-hearted discussions about the relationship itself can illuminate areas of growth and celebrate strengths. Such meta-communication—talking about how you talk—can reveal patterns and habits that either serve or hinder the relationship. By committing to an ongoing dialogue about the dynamics of your communication, you ensure that you're continually moving towards deeper mutual understanding and respect. This proactive approach guarantees that both partners feel valued and understood, laying down a resilient foundation for the future.

The Art of Setting and Respect Boundaries

In the fabric of healthy relationships, clear and respected boundaries serve as the threads keeping the connection strong and flexible. Understanding how to set and honor boundaries is not just about drawing lines around what we're comfortable with; it's about nurturing respect, trust, and open communication between individuals. Whether you're navigating the early stages of dating or deepening a long-term partnership, the ability to articulate your needs and listen to your partner's is foundational. This section dives into the nuances of boundary-setting—a skill that, when honed, enables both partners to thrive.

At the heart of effective boundary-setting is self-awareness. Before you can communicate what you need, it's crucial to invest time in understanding yourself. Reflect on your values, emotional needs, and the experiences that shape your comfort levels. This introspective work isn't always easy, but it's an essential step toward being able to articulate your boundaries clearly and assertively. Remember, boundaries can encompass a wide range of areas, including physical space, emotional intimacy, time spent together versus apart, and even digital communication patterns.

But setting boundaries is only half the equation; the other crucial component is respect. This involves actively listening when your partner communicates their boundaries and responding with understanding and flexibility. It's not uncommon for partners to have different boundary needs, and navigating these differences requires empathy and compromise. Respecting your partner's boundaries is a testament to your commitment to their well-being and the health of the relationship. It fosters a safe space where both partners feel valued and heard.

Conflict might arise when boundaries are crossed, intentionally or inadvertently. These moments, while challenging, also present opportunities for growth. Addressing boundary violations through calm, constructive conversation strengthens communication skills and deepens mutual understanding. It's about finding common ground and adjusting boundaries as the relationship evolves. Remember, the goal isn't to set rigid perimeters, but to cultivate a dynamic partnership where both individuals feel respected and free to be themselves.

In sum, the art of setting and respecting boundaries is crucial to building and maintaining healthy relationships. By fostering self-awareness, practicing open communication, and approaching differences with empathy, partners can create a supportive and resilient relationship. Boundaries, far from being barriers, are the building blocks of a strong, intimate connection. They allow us to navigate the complexities of human relationships with grace, ensuring that we not only grow as individuals but also as partners in a loving, balanced partnership.

Chapter 8

Self-Care

Rituals

Moving seamlessly from the foundations of setting healthy boundaries and effective communication, let's delve into a more personal realm— self-care rituals. It's pivotal, for the sake of your emotional well-being and the health of your future relationships, to carve out time for self- nurturing activities. Self-care isn't merely a buzzword tossed around in wellness circles; it's a crucial component of our mental and emotional health, directly impacting our interactions with others, including those we date or enter into relationships with.

Developing a self-care routine might sound daunting at first, especially if you're accustomed to putting others' needs before your own. However, starting small can lead to profound changes. Whether it's dedicating a few minutes each day to meditation, journaling, or simply enjoying a cup of coffee in silence, these rituals become sacred acts of self-love that replenish your emotional reservoir.

Mindfulness plays a significant role in self-care, acting as a bridge between our mental and physical well-being. In the fast-paced world we live in, our minds are often filled with clutter—be it from stress, digital overload, or the demands of daily life. Incorporating mindfulness techniques into your routine can help quiet the noise, allowing you to reconnect with yourself and the present moment. This, in turn, enhances your capacity to connect more authentically and deeply with others.

The beauty of self-care rituals is that they are deeply personal and can be tailored to fit anyone's lifestyle or needs. For some, vigorous exercise or hiking in nature serves as a powerful tool for clearing the mind and releasing pent-up energy. For others, creative expressions such as painting or writing provide a therapeutic outlet for emotions and stress. The key is to find activities that feel nourishing and fulfilling to you.

Beyond individual activities, self-care also encompasses how we treat our bodies on a basic level, including nutrition and rest. It's hard to understate the impact of a balanced diet and adequate sleep on our mood and energy levels. These fundamental aspects of self-care lay the groundwork for a healthier lifestyle, enabling us to show up as our best selves in relationships.

Remember, self-care is not selfish; it's a necessity. In the journey of building and maintaining healthy relationships, you must not lose sight of your well-being. The relationship you have with yourself sets the tone for every other relationship in your life. By nurturing this primary connection, you ensure that you're not only ready but also resilient enough to navigate the complexities of relationships with others.

As you forge ahead, consider the rituals you can institute or improve in your self-care routine. Take note of how these changes affect not just your relationship with yourself, but also how you relate to and connect with others. You might find that as you become more attuned and kinder to yourself, your capacity for empathy, understanding, and love in your relationships deepens as well.

Let these self-care rituals be your anchor amid the ebbs and flows of relationships and dating. They are your personal sanctuary; a place to return to for grounding and rejuvenation. As you continue to evolve and grow, your self-care practices too will change, reflecting your journey not just in the realm of love, but in the lifelong relationship you're building with yourself.

In the next chapter, we will venture into the world of dating with a fresh perspective. Armed with a strong sense of self and fortified by your self-care practices, you'll be better equipped to navigate the exciting, yet sometimes turbulent waters of dating. Remember, the path to finding love is also a path of self-discovery and growth, with self-care as your trusted companion along the way.

Developing a Self-Care Routine

As we embark on the venture of bolstering our relationships, it becomes crucial to underline the significance of self-care. It's a term that seems to buzz around every corner of our lives, urging us to slow down and pay heed to our own well-being. But how does one actually go about weaving a self-care routine into the fabric of their daily life? It's less about occasional indulgences and more about establishing practices that nourish you both on the surface and at the core.

Firstly, identifying what truly makes you feel rested, rejuvenated, and respected by your own self is a cornerstone. This could range from physical activities that boost your endorphins, like yoga or running, to more serene practices such as meditation or journaling. It's important to remember that self-care isn't a one-size-fits-all; what works wonders for one individual might not resonate with another. Experimentation and self-reflection are key in finding what best serves your mental, emotional, and physical health.

Moreover, integrating self-care into your daily life doesn't have to be a daunting task. It can be as simple as setting aside a specific time each day for activities that replenish your spirit. Whether it's reading a book, taking a long bath, or preparing a meal that nourishes your body and soul, the act of making time for these things is a declaration of self-worth and an important step towards self-love. These moments allow you to pause and reconnect with yourself, ensuring you're not just surviving, but thriving.

Another aspect often overlooked in self-care routines is setting boundaries—both with others and with oneself. Recognizing the importance of saying 'no' to overcommitments that deplete your energy reserves is crucial. It's also essential to be mindful of the digital world's impact on your mental health and to give yourself permission to disconnect when needed. Remember, boundaries are not barriers but rather the guidelines that protect your well-being.

Last but certainly not least, consistency is the golden thread that ties your self-care routine together. Much like building muscle or learning a new skill, the benefits of self-care practices compound over time with regularity. It might feel challenging to keep at it, especially on days when your schedule is packed or your motivation is low. However, it's these very practices that can anchor you during turbulent times and provide a sense of stability and self-compassion. Embark on this journey of self-care with an open heart, knowing that it's not just an act of self-love, but a foundational pillar for healthier, happier relationships moving forward.

Mindfulness and Its Role in Relationships

Moving on from the transformative practices of developing a self-care routine, we delve into the intricate dance of mindfulness and its profound impact on relationships. Mindfulness, in essence, is the art of being completely present and fully engaged with whatever we're doing at the moment — free from distraction or judgment, and aware of our thoughts and feelings without getting caught up in them. This practice, though simple in theory, can drastically change how we perceive and interact in our relationships.

Incorporating mindfulness into your relationship entails a conscious effort to be present with your partner, to listen deeply without the intent to reply but to understand, and to acknowledge feelings without immediately reacting to them. It's about appreciating the moments you share together and acknowledging each other's needs and boundaries. This might mean taking a few deep breaths before responding to a tense situation or expressing gratitude for each other's presence every day. By being mindful, we cultivate a space where compassion and empathy flourish, laying down a fertile ground for a relationship to grow resiliently against the inevitable challenges it will face.

But why exactly is mindfulness so crucial in relationships? Well, it all boils down to the fact that our minds can easily become our own worst enemies. Caught up in the past or anxious about the future, we neglect the present - where our relationships actually exist. Mindfulness teaches us to break free from these patterns of mind-wandering and to cherish the here and now. This not only enhances our own well-being but also makes us more attentive and appreciative partners. Moreover, mindfulness practices, such as meditation, can reduce stress and anxiety, contributing to healthier, happier relationships.

Starting to practice mindfulness in your relationship doesn't require a monumental shift in your daily routine. It can be as simple as jointly dedicating a few minutes each day to meditate, going on mindful walks together, or having undistracted meals where you both focus solely on enjoying the food and each other's company. These acts nurture a shared mindfulness practice that can strengthen the bond between you and your partner, ensuring that you're both engaged in building a relationship that is not only healthy but also deeply fulfilling.

As we navigate through the ebbs and flows of relationships, mindfulness serves as an anchor, keeping us grounded and connected with our partners. It allows us to approach conflicts with a calm mind and a compassionate heart, leading to resolutions that are constructive rather than destructive. Ultimately, by embracing mindfulness, we open ourselves up to a level of intimacy and understanding that forms the cornerstone of any lasting, loving relationship.

Chapter 9

The Dating

World

Welcome to the chapter that serves as your gateway into the vibrant, often exhilarating, sometimes baffling world of dating. By now, you've taken significant strides on your journey of self-discovery, learned about the essence of maintaining your well-being, and understood the value of building a foundation within yourself that's not just solid, but also nourishing and full of love. Now, it's time to extend that journey outward, into the realm of connecting deeply with others, in the quest for companionship, understanding, and love.

Dating, in its most beautiful form, is an exploration not just of another human being, but also of yourself. Each person you meet brings with them a mirror in which aspects of you are reflected back. Sometimes, these reflections will fill you with joy and validation; other times, they might challenge you, push you towards growth, or even make you reconsider parts of your personality you took for granted. It's here, in the give and take of personal discovery, that the beauty of dating truly lies.

However, it's no secret that the dating world can also be daunting. Fear of rejection, the vulnerability required in opening up to someone new, and the uncertainties that come with navigating initial connections can be overwhelming. Let's not forget the perplexing domain of online dating, where choices seem endless and interactions can, at times, feel both impersonal and intensely intimate. Yet, armed with your newfound knowledge and understanding of yourself, you're better equipped to face these challenges head-on, with grace and confidence.

One important lesson from your journey so far is the significance of authenticity. In an age where so much of dating involves online profiles and curated snapshots of life, being genuine might seem countercultural. Yet, it's authenticity that resonates, attracting others who appreciate the 'real' you. Maintaining your sense of self in a world that often demands compromise is not just brave; it's also the quickest route to finding a connection that's true and lasting.

Another key aspect to remember as you navigate the dating world is the importance of maintaining your well-being. This means setting and respecting boundaries, practising self-care, and listening closely to your emotional needs. It's easy to lose oneself in the whirlwind of dating or a budding romance, but your relationship with yourself remains your primary and most enduring partnership. Honouring this relationship is not only crucial for your personal happiness but also sets the stage for healthy, fulfilling relationships with others.

The art of communication, a theme that runs through this book, is especially valuable in the dating world. Whether deciphering the nuances of text messaging or expressing your needs and desires openly, effective communication can help build connections rooted in transparency and mutual respect. Mastering this art can turn potential misunderstandings into opportunities for deeper connection and intimacy.

As you step into the dating scene, remember, rejection is not a reflection of your worth. It's simply an indication of mismatched needs or desires. The resilience you've cultivated will guide you through these moments, helping you to see each experience as a stepping stone towards the right person for you. Like much of what you've learned, dating is as much about the journey as it is about the destination. Each encounter, each shared laugh, and even each goodbye, enriches your understanding of love and companionship.

Finally, while this chapter opens the door to "The Dating World," remember, the subsequent chapters will build on this foundation. They'll delve deeper into selecting the right dating platform, handling rejection, spotting compatibility, and nurturing new relationships. Consider this chapter the beginning of a new, exciting phase of your journey, one filled with potential for love, discovery, and unparalleled self-growth.

So, as you step forward into this new chapter of your life, do so with the assurance that comes from knowing yourself deeply, the courage to express that self authentically, and the resilience to embrace all that lies ahead. This is not just about finding love with someone else; it's also a profound continuation of the love affair with yourself. Welcome to the dating world—it promises to be an adventure like no other.

Chapter 10
Stepping Into the Dating Scene

After laying a robust foundation of self-awareness and setting the scene for a healthy approach to relationships, it's time to venture into the dating world with confidence and clarity. Stepping into the dating scene can feel like navigating uncharted waters, yet, with the right mindset and tools, it turns into an exciting journey of connection and discovery. It's essential to carry forward the lessons and skills you've cultivated – understanding your emotional needs, communication styles, and boundaries – as these will serve as your compass. Choosing the right dating platform plays a critical role in this modern dating era, as it can greatly influence the type of connections you'll encounter. While the thought of first dates might stir a mix of anticipation and nerves, focusing on keeping it healthy and fun ensures that, regardless of the outcome, each experience contributes positively to your growth. Embrace dating not just as a quest for partnership but as an extension of your journey of self-discovery, where each interaction enriches your understanding of yourself and what you seek in a companion.

Choosing the Right Dating Platform for You

Diving into the world of online dating can be as exciting as it is overwhelming. The plethora of choices available can make selecting the right platform a daunting task. Yet, taking this step is a significant part of your journey towards fostering meaningful connections. It's vital to remember that each dating app or website caters to distinct audiences and seeks to fulfill various relationship goals, from casual encounters to long-term partnerships. The key is to align your personal objectives with the platform you choose.

To navigate through this maze, consider what you are truly seeking in a relationship at this juncture of your life. Reflect on your personal values, interests, and relationship goals. Are you looking for someone who shares your passion for travel, music, or perhaps someone with a similar lifestyle? Some platforms use sophisticated algorithms to match you based on compatibility metrics, which can be particularly beneficial if you're seeking more than just a superficial connection.

Moreover, understanding the demographic that different platforms cater to can immensely enhance your online dating experience. For instance, some sites are more popular among certain age groups, while others may be more inclusive of diverse genders and sexual orientations. Taking the time to research and select a platform that aligns with your age group and personal identity can increase your chances of finding a compatible match.

Privacy and safety are paramount when exploring online dating. It's essential to choose platforms that prioritize users' safety and are proactive in implementing measures to prevent harassment and scams. Read through the privacy policies and user testimonials to gauge how seriously a platform takes user security and what measures are in place to protect you. Remember, a reputable dating site or app should empower you to control what information you share and with whom.

Lastly, an often-overlooked aspect is evaluating the user experience and interface of the platform. A well-designed app or website that's user-friendly can make your online dating journey more enjoyable and less frustrating. Compatibility is not just about the people you meet; it's also about how seamlessly you can interact with the platform to meet those individuals. As you embark on this exciting phase of your life, choosing the right dating platform is not just a step towards finding someone; it's about taking charge of your journey and shaping it with intention and clarity.

First Dates: Keeping It Healthy and Fun

As we venture into the realm of first dates, it's pivotal to prioritize both your emotional well-being and the enjoyment of the experience. The anticipation of a first date can sometimes feel overwhelming, swathed in a mix of excitement and nervousness. It's perfectly natural. By focusing on keeping the encounter healthy and enjoyable, you set the stage for potential connection and, just as importantly, a positive experience irrespective of the outcome.

Initiating the first date with an open mind and an open heart is key. This isn't about evaluating every word or action through a lens of long-term compatibility—rather, it's an opportunity to learn about someone else and, equally, about your own preferences and comfort levels in new situations. Choose activities or venues that facilitate conversation and mutual enjoyment. Whether it's a quiet coffee shop, a walk through a bustling market, or a visit to a local museum, the setting can significantly influence the mood and flow of the date. Remember, fun dates are often the simplest ones, where pressure is low, and genuine connection can spontaneously ignite.

Navigating the intricacies of initial conversations can feel like a dance—one that's both exhilarating and a bit intimidating. Strive to maintain a balance between sharing about yourself and listening attentively. Genuine curiosity about the other person not only fosters a feeling of respect and interest but can also reveal common ground or intriguing differences. It's essential, however, to steer clear of controversial or overly personal topics on a first date; there will be plenty of time to delve into deeper subjects as your connection, hopefully, strengthens over time.

Setting healthy boundaries from the outset is also crucial for both parties' comfort and safety. This includes respecting each other's privacy, personal space, and differing views. Remember, a respectful date is a foundation upon which everything else can build. If at any point you feel uneasy, it's more than okay to gracefully end the date. Your well-being is paramount, and there's no obligation to stay if your instincts tell you otherwise.

Lastly, managing expectations is a delicate but necessary aspect of first dates. While it's natural to hope for a spark or a memorable connection, equating every first date with potential life-partner material can lead to unnecessary disappointment. Embrace the experience for what it is—a chance to meet someone new and, at the very least, learn something interesting. Regardless of the outcome, value the courage it takes to step into the unknown and the growth that comes from putting yourself out there. After all, every encounter, be it romantic or platonic, is a step forward on your journey of self-discovery and relationship building.

Chapter 11

Rejection and Resilience

As we pivot from preparing ourselves for the dating world to actually stepping into it, we're met with a reality that's often glossed over but universally felt: rejection. It's a sting that can shatter our confidence and darken our outlook on love. Yet, it's also a critical juncture where resilience can be built. This chapter delves into how we can handle rejection with grace, seeing it not as a reflection of our worth but as a natural part of the dating process. It's about shifting perspective, from viewing rejection as a personal failure to seeing it as an opportunity for growth and self-discovery.

Learning to navigate rejection mindfully involves understanding that it's not just about bouncing back but growing stronger. This means looking inward, acknowledging our feelings, and then gently guiding ourselves forward. It's about cultivating a kind of emotional agility - the ability to acknowledge hurt feelings, learn from them, and then adapt with a renewed sense of purpose. We'll explore techniques to not only survive rejections but to thrive in their aftermath, using them as stepping stones toward becoming more resilient, empathetic partners in future relationships.

Through this resilience, we also pave the way for more authentic connections. By shedding the fear of rejection, we allow our true selves to shine, attracting people who appreciate us for who we are. This chapter provides insight into turning what feels like dating's most disheartening moments into its most empowering lessons, ensuring we remain open, hopeful, and ever-evolving on our journey to love.

Handling Rejection Mindfully

Let's face it, rejection stings. Whether it's a swipe left or an unreturned text, each small or big instance can feel like a direct hit to your self-worth. However, it's crucial to remember that rejection is an inevitable part of the dating process, not a reflection of your value as a person. By approaching these experiences mindfully, you can transform them from soul-crushing defeats to opportunities for growth and self-reflection.

Firstly, when you face rejection, take a moment to acknowledge your feelings without judgment. It's okay to feel hurt, disappointed, or even angry. These are natural responses to not receiving something you hoped for. However, the key is not to dwell on these emotions. Allow yourself to experience them, then gently shift your focus to what you can learn from the situation.

Practicing mindfulness can play a significant role in this process. It involves staying present and fully engaging with your experiences without over-identifying with negative thoughts or emotions. When you're mindful, you recognize that while rejection is uncomfortable, it doesn't define you or your ability to find love and happiness.

Another helpful approach is to reframe how you view rejection. Instead of seeing it as a failure, consider it a step closer to finding someone who's truly right for you. Each rejection helps clarify what you're really looking for in a partner and can guide you in adjusting your search criteria or approach. This perspective doesn't just soften the blow of rejection; it transforms it into a tool for honing your understanding of your desires and needs in a relationship.

It's also beneficial to cultivate a strong support network of friends and family who can offer perspective and encouragement. Share your experiences with them and be open to their insights. Sometimes, an outside perspective can shed light on situations in ways you hadn't considered, making the process of dealing with rejection less isolating.

Furthermore, keeping a journal can be a therapeutic way to process your feelings and track your personal growth. Writing about your experiences with rejection, your reactions, and how you're working through them not only helps in managing emotions but also in noticing patterns that may be worth addressing.

Additionally, focusing on self-improvement can be a constructive response to rejection. Whether it's picking up a new hobby, enhancing your skills, or simply dedicating time to self-care, investing in yourself boosts your self-esteem and resilience. It serves as a reminder that your happiness and value come from within, not from someone else's acceptance or approval.

Remember, resilience doesn't mean becoming numb to rejection or pretending it doesn't hurt. Instead, it's about developing a robust internal compass that guides you through the ups and downs of dating. It's about learning that you can encounter rejection and not only survive but thrive, emerging more grounded and self-assured on the other side.

Lastly, always practice compassion towards yourself. Be as kind and understanding to yourself in moments of rejection as you would be to a dear friend in the same situation. Self-compassion is a powerful tool in healing and moving forward. It strengthens your emotional resilience, allowing you to bounce back more quickly and with a more positive outlook on your journey towards finding meaningful connections.

In summary, while rejection will likely always be a part of the dating landscape, it doesn't have to derail your pursuit of love and connection. By handling rejection mindfully, you can minimize its impact, learn valuable lessons, and continue moving forward with confidence and clarity. Remember, every experience, even those that seem negative, is an opportunity to grow closer to the person you are meant to be with — yourself first and, eventually, your ideal partner.

Learning and Growing from Dating Experiences

Diving into the world of dating often leads us through a rollercoaster of emotions, filled with highs of excitement and lows of disappointments. It's these very experiences, however, that hold invaluable lessons about love, resilience, and self-discovery. As we navigate through different relationships and encounters, each one offers a unique opportunity for growth and reflection. Understanding this helps us transform the way we view dating – not just as a search for a partner but as a journey towards becoming our best selves.

When we embark on this voyage, it's inevitable to face rejection and heartbreak. Rather than seeing these moments as failures, it's crucial to reframe them as stepping stones. Each interaction that doesn't work out is guiding us closer to understanding what we truly desire in a partner. This reframing is not just about optimism; it's about recognizing the strength and resilience we build each time we pick ourselves up after a setback.

Reflecting on our dating experiences allows us to identify patterns in our choices and behaviors. Are we drawn to similar types of people, and if so, why? Do certain behaviors or traits in partners trigger negative reactions in us? These reflections can shine a light on our own emotional needs and insecurities, helping us to address and heal them. As we grow to understand these aspects of ourselves, we become better equipped to choose partners who truly complement and support us.

A crucial part of learning from our dating experiences is the practice of self-compassion. Being kind to ourselves in moments of rejection or failed relationships helps mitigate the impact of these moments on our self-esteem. Recognizing that each experience is a part of our journey, rather than a reflection of our worth, enables us to maintain a healthy perspective on dating.

It's also essential to celebrate the successes, no matter how small they might seem. Whether it's having an enjoyable conversation, feeling a spark with someone new, or simply getting out there and trying, these moments are victories in their own right. Acknowledging and celebrating these successes fosters a sense of positivity and momentum in our dating lives.

Setting boundaries is another critical lesson from our dating experiences. Learning to say no, expressing our needs clearly, and respecting our boundaries, as well as others', are fundamental skills in building healthy relationships. Through trial and error, we learn what we are comfortable with and how to communicate these boundaries assertively and respectfully.

Finally, embracing vulnerability is perhaps one of the most profound ways we can grow from dating. Allowing ourselves to be seen and to see others, with all our imperfections and weaknesses, fosters genuine connections. Vulnerability might seem frightening, but it's also the pathway to deep, meaningful relationships. Each dating experience, then, becomes a practice in courage as we learn to open our hearts a little more each time.

In the journey of dating, it's the lessons we learn about ourselves that are the most precious. Our experiences teach us about our capacity for love, resilience, and self-reflection. They remind us that while not every encounter will lead to lasting love, each one is a step towards understanding ourselves and what it means to connect deeply with another person.

So, as we continue to navigate the dating world, let's approach it with curiosity, openness, and a willingness to learn from each experience. By doing so, we're not just searching for the right partner; we're also building ourselves into someone ready for the deep, fulfilling relationship we desire. And that is perhaps the most valuable outcome of our dating adventures.

Remember, the goal of dating isn't just to find someone who fits into our lives; it's also about growing into the person who is ready for that special someone when they come along. As we learn and grow from each dating experience, we're also preparing ourselves for the rich, rewarding relationship that awaits us. In this way, every step of the journey is invaluable, teaching us lessons that enrich our lives in ways we might never have imagined.

Chapter 12

Spotting Compatibility

A crucial, yet often overlooked, aspect of building a strong, healthy relationship is spotting compatibility early on. You've spent several chapters exploring and understanding your own needs, desires, and emotional landscapes. Now, it's time to apply that understanding to gauge the fit between you and potential partners. Compatibility isn't about having identical interests or the same taste in music, though those can be nice bonuses. At its core, it's about aligning on the deeper, fundamental levels – your core values and beliefs. This alignment doesn't mean you agree on everything, but it does mean you share a common foundation that governs how you see the world.

One of the key indicators of this kind of deep-seated match is recognizing emotional availability in yourself and your potential partner. Emotional availability encompasses the willingness and ability to share feelings openly, to engage with the emotions of others, and to commit to the sometimes messy process of building intimacy. It's the difference between a partner who deflects and avoids when topics get too real and one who meets challenges and vulnerabilities with empathy. Spotting emotional availability early helps set the stage for developing a relationship where both partners feel seen, valued, and understood.

But how exactly can you spot compatibility and emotional availability? Pay attention to how conversations unfold, the questions they ask, and the level of interest they show in truly understanding you. It's also in the way disagreements are managed - are they an opportunity for growth or a battleground? Remember, a key part of being ready to date is not just knowing what you want, but what you are prepared to give. As you continue your journey in the dating world, carry with you the insights you've learned so far, along with your openness to learn and grow. Spotting compatibility is not about finding a perfect match but recognizing the right connection that encourages mutual growth, respect, and affection.

Aligning Core Values and Beliefs

In our journey through the landscape of building and nurturing relationships, we've explored various aspects critical to the formation of a robust, healthy partnership. As we delve into the essence of spotting compatibility, it's essential to focus on the alignment of core values and beliefs between partners. This chapter is aimed at guiding you on how to navigate this crucial aspect of compatibility, which often acts as the backbone of lasting relationships.

Understanding the significance of shared values and beliefs cannot be overstated. They are the silent undercurrents that influence our decisions, our behaviors, and how we interact with the world and our partner. When two individuals share a common ground in their core values, they find a familiar and comforting resonance in how they view and approach life. It's like moving to the rhythm of the same beat, even when the music changes.

Core values and beliefs span a wide range: from notions of right and wrong, spiritual or religious beliefs, to perspectives on family, money, and the pursuit of happiness. They shape our expectations in a relationship and the future we envision with our partner. When these values are aligned, it fosters an environment where mutual respect flourishes, and differences can be navigated with empathy and understanding.

It's worth noting, however, that alignment doesn't necessitate identical values and beliefs. Rather, it's about the harmony in differences that can coexist without conflict. For instance, two people might have different religious beliefs but share a common value in the importance of spirituality, allowing them to respect and support each other's spiritual paths.

Finding this alignment begins with introspection. It's about gaining clarity on your own core values and beliefs. Recalling the exercises in previous chapters, you've embarked on a journey of self-discovery, identifying your emotional needs and understanding your personality. These insights serve as a foundation for recognizing what you value most in life and, subsequently, in a partner.

Communication plays a pivotal role in this discovery process within the dating context. Engaging in open, honest conversations about topics that touch upon your core values can reveal much about your compatibility with a potential partner. These discussions can range from your aspirations, ethical dilemmas you've faced, to your definitions of success and happiness. Such conversations not only deepen your understanding of each other but also build a bridge of closeness and trust.

Moreover, observing actions and decisions can be as telling as words. As the saying goes, "Actions speak louder than words." In the course of dating, pay attention to how your date's actions reflect their stated values and beliefs. Consistency between words and actions is a telling sign of integrity and authenticity, qualities that are indispensable in a healthy relationship.

It's also important to be mindful of the difference between superficial preferences and core values. While having similar interests and hobbies can enhance your connection, it's the alignment in core values that sustains a relationship through life's inevitable challenges and changes. Thus, focusing on deep compatibility rather than surface-level commonalities is key to forging a lasting bond.

In essence, aligning core values and beliefs with your partner is akin to building a strong, resilient structure that can withstand the tests of time. It anchors your relationship in a shared vision of life and nurtures a profound understanding and respect for each other. As you progress in your dating journey, let this alignment be your guide in choosing a partner with whom you can grow and flourish together.

Remember, the path to finding a compatible partner who shares your core values and beliefs is also a journey of growth and discovery for yourself. Embrace this journey with an open heart and mind, and let the shared values illuminate your path toward a fulfilling, lasting relationship.

Recognizing Emotional Availability

As we make our way through the intricate maze of dating and relationships, one quality stands out as crucial for establishing a profound connection: emotional availability. But what does it really mean to be emotionally available? It means being open and ready to share feelings, to connect deeply with another person, and to be present in the relationship without walls or barriers.

This concept might sound straightforward, but identifying emotional availability in a potential partner can be challenging. It requires attentiveness, intuition, and, most importantly, a solid understanding of one's own emotional state. The foundation for recognizing emotional availability in others is being emotionally available yourself. When you are open and honest about your feelings, it becomes easier to see when others are doing the same.

One of the first signs of emotional availability is effective communication. An emotionally available person doesn't just talk; they listen. They're not only sharing their thoughts and feelings but are genuinely interested in hearing yours. It's this mutual exchange that deepens the connection and fosters intimacy.

Another indicator is vulnerability. Being vulnerable means opening up and sharing the parts of yourself that aren't so polished - your fears, dreams, and disappointments. It's about letting someone into the more intimate aspects of your life. When someone is willing to show their vulnerability, it's a powerful sign of emotional openness.

Consistency is also key in spotting emotional availability. Emotionally available people show a consistent pattern in their behavior towards you and others. Their actions match their words. This consistency provides a sense of security and trust, which are essential for a healthy relationship.

Responsiveness to emotional cues is crucial as well. Emotionally available people are attuned to the feelings of others. They can sense when you're upset or joyful and respond appropriately. This emotional attunement fosters a deep sense of empathy and understanding within the relationship.

It's also important to remember that emotional availability isn't static; it can fluctuate. Life's stressors and challenges can momentarily make someone less open and available. Recognizing this is important in nurturing patience and understanding within the relationship.

That said, a consistent pattern of emotional unavailability is a red flag. It may indicate unresolved personal issues or a lack of readiness for a deep connection. While it's essential to be supportive, it's also crucial to recognize when emotional unavailability is a barrier to a healthy, fulfilling relationship.

Finally, recognizing emotional availability in others starts with a journey of self-discovery and affirming your own emotional health. By cultivating your emotional availability, you set the stage for meaningful connections. It's not just about finding the right person; it's about being the right person.

In essence, emotional availability encompasses both the capacity to share and to listen, to offer support, and to seek it. It's about building a bridge between self and other, fostering a connection that is both deep and enduring. As we navigate the path to love, let's aspire to be emotionally available, to ourselves and to those we invite into our hearts.

Chapter 13

Nurturing New Relationships

As we transition from the exhilarating initial phases of dating to the somewhat more stable grounds of a new relationship, the focus subtly shifts. It's no longer just about sparking interest and navigating first dates but about cultivating a connection that has the potential to last. Nurturing a new relationship involves a delicate blend of patience, openness, and dedication. While the fireworks of the early days are magical in their own right, the gradual building of trust and intimacy paves the way for a deeper, more meaningful bond.

One key aspect of nurturing a new relationship is maintaining effective communication. It's essential to foster an environment where both partners feel heard and understood. This means not only sharing your own thoughts and feelings but actively listening to your partner's perspective. Honest and open dialogue can significantly strengthen the connection, helping to build a foundation of trust and mutual respect. Through this, you can learn a great deal more about each other, exploring beliefs, dreams, and even fears together.

Another vital element is patience. Understand that true intimacy and understanding don't develop overnight. Every relationship progresses at its own pace, and it's crucial to respect that timeline. Rushing can create unnecessary pressure and might even lead to misunderstandings or conflicts that could have been avoided. It's okay to take your time, allowing both you and your partner to comfortably grow into the relationship without feeling overwhelmed.

Setting boundaries is also an important part of nurturing a new relationship. Boundaries help define what you're comfortable with and how you'd like to be treated, fostering a safe and respectful environment for both partners. It's crucial to communicate these boundaries clearly and respect those set by your partner. This not only minimizes the potential for conflict but also deepens understanding and empathy between you both.

Investing in shared experiences can further strengthen the bond. Whether it's trying new activities together, exploring mutual interests, or simply setting aside quality time to connect, shared experiences can create lasting memories and strengthen the relationship. These moments don't always have to be grand or expensive; sometimes, it's the simple acts of togetherness that mean the most and nurture the bond in profound ways.

However, maintaining your individuality within the relationship is equally important. It's easy to get caught up in the whirlwind of a new romance and lose sight of yourself. Remember, a healthy relationship is made up of two whole individuals who bring their unique selves to the partnership. Encourage each other to pursue personal interests and goals, as this will not only lead to personal growth but also bring fresh energy and perspectives into the relationship.

Finally, facing challenges together can significantly contribute to nurturing a new relationship. It's inevitable that you'll encounter obstacles along the way, but how you address them can either strengthen or weaken the bond. Approach challenges as a team, working together to find solutions. This not only helps resolve the issue at hand but also demonstrates commitment and resilience, key components of a lasting relationship.

Throughout this journey, it's crucial to stay mindful and present. Appreciate the small moments, the everyday gestures of love and care. It's these little things that often mean the most and contribute significantly to the relationship's growth. So while you're focusing on building a future together, don't forget to cherish the present, the here and now, for it's the foundation upon which everything else is built.

In nurturing a new relationship, patience, communication, and mutual respect are paramount. Remember, it's about building something beautiful together, gradually, with each passing day. Each step taken together is a step toward a deeper connection, a partnership that's not only fulfilling but also enriching in every sense. So keep nurturing your budding relationship with care, thoughtfulness, and love, knowing that these early days are just the beginning of a wonderful journey ahead.

As we move forward to the next chapter, we'll delve into the progression of healthy dating, understanding the phases of a relationship, and how to balance the heart and head. This knowledge will further guide you in nurturing your relationship, helping it evolve in a healthy and positive direction.

Chapter 14
The Progression of Healthy Dating

As we gently navigate the waters from nurturing new relationships towards the more intricate dynamics of dating, it's crucial to understand that the progression of healthy dating isn't linear, nor is it a one-size-fits-all journey. It comprises various phases, each marked by its own set of experiences, learning curves, and moments of introspection. A significant part of this journey involves striking a delicate balance between listening to your heart and using your head. This equilibrium enables one to make thoughtful decisions, recognize potential red flags early, and foster a relationship that's not just thrilling but also grounded in mutual respect and understanding.

Healthy dating progresses through phases where individuals learn more about each other, dive deeper into their shared interests, and confront, with kindness and patience, the inevitable differences that surface. It's a time when couples start to navigate the complexities of vulnerability, gradually opening up and building trust. The pace at which this happens can vary greatly, and that's okay. One of the most beautiful aspects of healthy dating is its capacity to tailor itself to the unique needs and rhythms of the individuals involved. It's about finding joy in the moments you share, learning from disagreements, and growing together, all the while maintaining a sense of identity and pursuing personal goals. Drawing upon the depth of self-knowledge and emotional resilience cultivated in earlier chapters, this stage of dating becomes an enriching experience that contributes to personal growth and paves the way for a fulfilling partnership.

Understanding the Phases of Dating

Embarking on the journey of dating can feel like navigating through a dense fog without a compass. However, understanding the natural progression of healthy dating can clear the mist, guiding you towards fulfilling relationships. Dating is not a linear process, but it typically moves through recognizable phases that help deepen connection and intimacy between partners. Let's explore these phases, with the aim of providing clarity and confidence in your dating experiences.

The initial phase of dating, often termed the 'attraction phase,' is characterized by an intense focus on the physical and emotional appeal of a potential partner. It's a time filled with excitement, anticipation, and, often, a fair amount of nervousness. During this stage, it's common to idealize the other person, overlooking potential flaws and red flags in the thrill of new romance. Mindfulness can be particularly valuable here, helping you stay grounded and focused on your core values and emotional needs.

As the relationship progresses, you enter the 'reality phase.' This is when the haze of infatuation starts to lift, and both individuals' true selves begin to emerge. It's a critical time for communication and honesty, as understanding each other's personalities, goals, and emotional needs becomes paramount. This phase often tests the resilience and compatibility of the relationship, providing important insights into whether the partnership can withstand the trials of real life.

Following the reality check comes the 'commitment phase,' where both partners make a conscious decision to work through challenges together. This isn't about losing oneself in the relationship; rather, it's about building a partnership that respects individuality while fostering mutual growth and support. Communication, trust, and boundary-setting are key components during this stage. It offers an opportunity to deepen the connection by navigating life's ups and downs as a team, reinforcing the relationship's foundation.

Finally, there's the 'deepening phase,' marked by increased trust, security, and intimacy. Partners in this phase often feel a strong bond, having navigated the highs and lows of the previous stages together. It's a time for building a shared future, yet it also emphasizes the importance of maintaining individual identities and personal growth. Healthy relationships allow for both closeness and personal space, encouraging each individual to pursue their own goals and interests while supporting each other.

Understanding these phases of dating can equip you with the insight needed to navigate your dating journey with more grace and confidence. It's important to remember that each relationship is unique; while these phases offer a general framework, your experience may vary. Stay true to your values, communicate openly, and practice self-care throughout your dating adventures. By doing so, you'll be well-positioned to forge meaningful, lasting connections.

Balancing Heart and Head

As we delve deeper into the progression of healthy dating, a crucial topic emerges: the balance between heart and head. It's akin to walking a tightrope, where even the slightest tilt might throw us off. In the realm of dating, we often find ourselves tugged in one direction by our emotions and pulled in another by our rational thoughts. This section is a guide to navigating these forces with grace, ensuring you stay true to yourself while fully embracing the experience of connecting with another.

First, let's address the heart - our emotional center. It's what makes us human, capable of love, empathy, and deep connection. When we start dating someone new, it's our heart that often speaks first, urging us to leap. It's the voice that tells us there's something special here, the flutter we feel when receiving a message from that person, and the warmth that spreads through us with their smile. This emotional guidance is precious; it's the seed from which love can blossom. However, when left unchecked, our heart can lead us into whirlwinds of unbalanced relationships, or have us wearing rose-colored glasses, ignoring potential red flags.

On the flip side, we have the head - our logical center. It's the part of us that asks questions, analyzes compatibility, and considers the long-term potential of our connections. The head helps us step back and view our budding relationship from a broader perspective. It reminds us of our priorities, personal goals, and the lessons learned from past relationships. This analytical approach is equally invaluable. It protects us from potential hurt and ensures we're aligning with partners who truly fit into the life we envision for ourselves. Yet, if we let it take over, we risk becoming overly critical or creating barriers that prevent genuine connection.

Finding equilibrium between heart and head isn't a simple task; it's a dynamic process that evolves with each new relationship experience. It starts with self-awareness, recognizing when you're leaning too much to one side and consciously bringing yourself back to center. It involves listening deeply to both your emotions and your thoughts, acknowledging each without letting either dominate. Communication plays a crucial role here - not only with your partner but also with yourself. It's important to regularly check in, asking how you feel and what you think about the direction your relationship is heading.

An effective way to balance heart and head is setting aside time for reflection after dates or significant interactions with your partner. Consider what your emotions are telling you and what your logical mind advises. Are they in conflict, or do they complement each other? Reflection helps us understand our true desires and assess whether our relationship dynamics align with them.

Balancing heart and head also means being open to both joys and disappointments. Embrace vulnerability by allowing yourself to feel, but take wisdom's hand, letting it guide you through uncertainties. It's about trusting the process, knowing that each experience, whether a heart flutter or a moment of doubt, is a step towards a deeper understanding of yourself and what you seek in a partner.

Relationships that find this balance tend to be healthier and more fulfilling. Such partnerships are built not only on emotional connection but also on a mutual respect for individual needs, dreams, and aspirations. They are relationships where both partners feel heard and understood, able to express their feelings without fear, while also considering practical aspects of building a life together.

As you move forward in your dating journey, keep the balance between heart and head at the forefront of your mind. It's a delicate dance, but one that enriches the fabric of our relationships, weaving together threads of passion and pragmatism. Allow yourself to love boldly, but also love wisely, nurturing connections that uplift and support you in every way.

Ultimately, the journey of dating is not just about finding the right partner; it's about growing as an individual. It's about learning to navigate the complexities of human emotions and interactions, discovering how to harmonize the divergent voices within us. In striking the balance between heart and head, we don't just become better partners; we become more integrated, balanced individuals - capable of both deep feeling and thoughtful action.

Embrace this challenge with an open heart and a clear mind. It's in this balance that the true beauty of a relationship unfolds, revealing a path to genuine, lasting connections. As you continue to explore the vast panorama of dating, let the equilibrium between your heart and head be your guiding light, leading you to the love and partnership you seek and deserve.

Chapter 15

Intimacy and Vulnerability

Moving forward from the fertile grounds of healthy dating into the realms of deeper connection, we pivot to the cornerstone of lasting relationships: intimacy and vulnerability. Intimacy, in its purest form, isn't just about physical closeness; it's about feeling fully seen, understood, and accepted. But here's the catch – to foster intimacy, one must be willing to navigate the less comfortable terrain of vulnerability. This involves slowly peeling away the layers of our persona, revealing our true selves, inclusive of our fears, dreams, and sometimes, the shadows of our past. It's a delicate dance between two souls, wherein each step closer can feel like a leap into the unknown.

Trust doesn't emerge overnight. It's built incrementally, with each shared experience, conversation, and display of affection or support laying down the bricks. As we venture through this chapter, we explore strategies to build trust in a pace that feels right, respecting both your boundaries and those of your partner. It's about finding that sweet spot where sharing becomes not just an act of revealing but an opportunity for connection and growth. Safe-sharing practices are paramount; not every detail needs to be divulged all at once. It's akin to turning the pages of a book you both are writing together – each page a step deeper into the heart of your collective narrative.

Yet, the path of vulnerability is fraught with the risk of hurt – it's an inherent part of the process. Herein lies the strength of vulnerability in intimacy: it invites us to confront our fears and insecurities in the presence of someone who cares, paving the way for healing and deeper

connection. Embracing vulnerability is not a sign of weakness but a testament to the strength of human connection. As we delve into the nuances of fostering intimacy and navigating vulnerabilities safely, remember this journey isn't about losing yourself to the relationship but enriching it by sharing the most authentic version of you. In doing so, you and your partner create a foundation not just of love, but of unwavering trust and understanding.

Building Trust Incrementally

Trust, an essential building block of any intimate relationship, doesn't emerge fully formed; it develops over time. It's akin to laying bricks for a pathway, where each brick represents moments and experiences shared between two people. When embarking on a new relationship, the idea of opening up can seem daunting. You may feel vulnerable, uncertain how much of yourself to reveal, and when. It's a dance that requires patience, understanding, and, most crucially, the ability to listen and empathize with each other.

Initiating this journey begins with small steps. Sharing minor personal disclosures, like your interests, preferences, or funny anecdotes from your childhood, opens the door to deeper conversations. It's these moments, seemingly inconsequential, that set the foundation for trust. This doesn't mean you should rush to share your deepest, most personal secrets early on. Rather, it's about building a sense of comfort and safety with your partner, where both parties feel heard and respected.

As trust grows, so does the depth of the topics you explore together. Discussing fears, dreams, and even past relationship challenges can strengthen the bond between you and your partner. However, it's essential to gauge the readiness of both individuals to delve into more sensitive subjects. Mutual readiness creates a safe space for vulnerability, minimizing the risk of feeling exposed or judged. It's a delicate balance, ensuring that neither partner feels pressured to reveal more than they're comfortable with.

Remember, setbacks in building trust are normal and can be part of the process. Misunderstandings and disagreements present opportunities for growth if handled with care, respect, and open communication. When issues arise, addressing them directly and honestly can prevent erosion of the trust you've both worked hard to establish. It's through navigating these challenges together that trust is not only built but fortified.

Ultimately, trust is not just about believing in your partner's honesty or faithfulness. It's about feeling secure enough to be your true selves around each other. This security doesn't materialize overnight; it evolves through shared experiences, consistent communication, and the mutual willingness to be vulnerable. By building trust incrementally, you create a resilient, profound connection that can withstand the tests and trials of a relationship.

Sharing Vulnerabilities Safely

In the realm of building deep, meaningful connections, the act of sharing vulnerabilities stands as a cornerstone. It's a profound way to foster trust and intimacy, yet it's equally fraught with fears of rejection or misunderstanding. Thus, navigating this delicate terrain requires thoughtfulness and courage. It's pivotal to open up in a manner that safeguards your emotional well-being while allowing your relationship to deepen authentically.

First and foremost, assess the foundation you've built with your partner so far. Trust and mutual respect are non-negotiable prerequisites for safe vulnerability sharing. It's less about the duration of the relationship and more about the quality of the interactions and the strength of the trust you've cultivated. If these elements are in place, you're more likely to find a receptive and supportive listener in your partner.

Timing plays an essential role as well. While there's no perfect moment to bare your soul, choosing a serene, private setting where both you and your partner are relaxed and free from distractions can make a substantial difference. Such an environment not only facilitates deeper listening but also underscores the significance of what you're about to share.

It's also useful to start small. Sharing vulnerabilities is not an all-or-nothing endeavor. Begin with less intense disclosures and gradually work your way up as your comfort level and confidence in your partner's reactions grow. This approach helps build a robust scaffolding for more significant revelations in the future.

Expressing your feelings and experiences clearly and calmly is key. It's tempting to downplay your emotions or rush through your story, but such tactics can dilute the significance of your vulnerability. Instead, strive for clarity and honesty, and allow your partner the time to process and respond.

Furthermore, it's crucial to manage your expectations. While hope for understanding and empathy is natural, it's important to prepare for a variety of responses. Your partner might need time to digest your revelations or may have questions. Their initial reaction is not an absolute indicator of the depth of their care for you or the future of your relationship.

Listening to your partner's vulnerabilities with the same openness and support you seek is equally important. Sharing vulnerabilities is a two-way street that can significantly strengthen your bond if navigated with mutual respect and compassion.

In case of a negative outcome, such as a mismatch in expectations or a realization that the relationship might not be as solid as hoped, it's vital to approach the situation with self-compassion. Viewing the experience as a step towards finding a more compatible partner or as a learning opportunity can ease the sting of disappointment.

To further facilitate this delicate exchange, consider establishing a ritual or a specific phrase that signals your need to share something deeply personal. This can help both partners mentally prepare for a serious conversation, ensuring that vulnerabilities are approached with the gravity and care they deserve.

Lastly, remember that sharing vulnerabilities is an ongoing journey, not a one-time task. As your relationship evolves, so will the depths of your shared intimacies. Each step taken towards openness and honesty is a step towards a richer, more fulfilling partnership.

Chapter 16

Maintaining Your

Identity

Maintaining your identity amidst the whirlwind of a new romance isn't just important; it's essential for the health and longevity of both you and your relationship. It's easy to get caught up in the bliss of a blossoming partnership, where suddenly all your plans have a plus one and your individual routines start to blend. However, the importance of pursuing personal goals while dating cannot be stressed enough. You've built a life you're proud of, filled with personal achievements and ongoing ambitions. Keeping sight of these not only nurtures your sense of self but also enriches the bond you're creating with your partner, offering fresh experiences and growth opportunities for both of you.

A relationship, while being a union, is, in essence, a partnership between two distinct individuals who have their unique perspectives, interests, and aspirations. Investing in personal and shared interests is a balancing act that encourages respect and admiration between partners. It's about finding joy and fulfillment in your activities outside the relationship, which in turn, brings positive energy and new experiences into the relationship. This balance prevents the relationship from becoming the sole focus of your life, which can lead to pressure and eventually resentment. It's vital to remember that the relationship is just one aspect of your richly layered life.

Communication plays a pivotal role in maintaining your identity within a relationship. It's crucial to express your needs and desires to your partner openly. This includes discussing the importance of alone time, or time spent with friends or on hobbies. It's okay to have different interests; in fact, it's healthy. Encouraging each other to pursue these can strengthen your bond. You might discover a newfound appreciation for your partner as you witness them in their element, pursuing what they love. Additionally, this space and independence foster trust and confidence within the relationship, which are pillars of a strong partnership.

Finding a harmony between togetherness and individuality might seem daunting at first. It requires effort, understanding, and sometimes, compromise. But it is deeply rewarding. Celebrating each other's successes and supporting one another during setbacks, while also thriving in your personal endeavors, cultivates a profound respect. This mutual support system ensures the relationship thrives, grounded in mutual admiration and individual strength. Remember, a relationship where both partners are encouraged to grow independently is one where love blossoms most healthily.

In the end, maintaining your identity in a relationship boils down to staying true to yourself while nurturing the bond you're building together. It's about continuing to love and invest in yourself as much as you do in your relationship. This way, you're not just partners; you're allies on this journey of life, celebrating every step of your personal and shared paths. By fostering your independence and supporting each other's growth, you create a relationship that is both vibrant and resilient, capable of withstanding the tests of time while remaining ever dynamic and fulfilling.

Pursuing Personal Goals While Dating

As you embark on the exciting journey of dating, it's easy to get wrapped up in the whirlwind of romance and new connections. Yet, it's crucial to remember that maintaining your identity and pursuing personal goals are integral to a healthy and fulfilling relationship.

Just as we've navigated through understanding ourselves, past patterns, and future dreams, bringing our whole selves to a relationship includes our aspirations outside of it.

While navigating the delicate balance of sharing your life with someone and maintaining your personal journey, setting boundaries around your goals becomes an act of self-care. It's about knowing when to say yes to a weekend work project that excites you or a solo adventure that fuels your soul. It's acknowledging that personal growth and relationship growth can, and should, coexist harmoniously. By communicating your needs and aspirations to your partner, you're not building walls but rather, bridges to mutual respect and understanding.

Investing time in your hobbies, career, and personal projects isn't a luxury; it's a necessity. It's what keeps you vibrant, engaged, and true to yourself. Diving into these passions doesn't detract from your relationship; it enriches it. You bring fresh ideas, energy, and inspiration to the table, which can, in turn, inspire your partner and strengthen your bond. After all, a partnership thrives when both individuals are thriving.

Moreover, pursuing personal goals while dating sets a foundation for a resilient relationship. Life throws challenges our way—career changes, health issues, and family matters. When both partners are accustomed to supporting each other's personal journeys, navigating these waters together becomes less daunting. You become each other's cheerleader, confidant, and stable ground, knowing well how to balance the scales of personal needs and collective responsibilities.

Remember, the pursuit of personal goals isn't a solitary journey taken away from your relationship, but rather, a parallel path that complements it. Each step you take towards your dreams adds another layer of depth, understanding, and respect to your relationship. By maintaining your identity and continuing to pursue what makes you uniquely you, the relationship you are building with another becomes all the more enriching and profound.

Investing in Personal and Shared Interests

Maintaining your identity within the tapestry of a relationship is akin to walking a tightrope. It requires balance, concentration, and, most importantly, the courage to invest in both your personal interests and those you share with your partner. It's easy to get caught up in the whirlwind of a new relationship. Suddenly, you find every waking moment is spent or planned with your significant other. However, retaining your individuality is crucial for a healthy, balanced relationship. By investing time in your personal interests, you pave the way for personal growth, which in turn enriches your relationship.

Personal interests act as a sanctuary for your identity. They're the hobbies, passions, and pursuits that light you up inside and make you, well, *you*. Continuing to engage with these activities while in a relationship not only maintains your sense of self but also brings new experiences and insights into your partnership. Imagine sharing the excitement of mastering a new skill or discovering a hidden talent with your partner. It adds layers of depth to conversations and can ignite a spark of admiration and attraction that goes beyond the superficial.

Similarly, investing in shared interests can be equally rewarding. Shared interests create a common ground, a space where both partners can engage, learn, and grow together. It's about finding activities that both of you are passionate about or curious to explore. Perhaps it's cooking classes, hiking, or volunteering for a cause close to both your hearts. These shared experiences can strengthen your bond and provide countless memories and stories to cherish.

However, merging your hobbies shouldn't mean losing sight of your individual interests. It's about striking a balance—allocating time for personal pursuits alongside shared activities. Communication plays a pivotal role here. It's important to express your desires and listen to your partner's, ensuring that both of you feel heard and supported in your individual and collective growth.

Interestingly, investing in both personal and shared interests can significantly enhance your relationship's quality. With personal interests, you bring back stories, skills, and experiences to share with your partner, keeping the relationship dynamic and engaging. On the other hand, shared interests provide a platform for collaborative growth, deepening your connection and understanding of each other.

It might seem challenging at first, especially if you're used to spending most of your time with your partner. However, setting boundaries and scheduling can greatly help. Dedicate certain days or hours to your personal interests and others to shared activities. It's like planning dates with yourself and your partner. The anticipation of these moments can be quite exhilarating and refreshing for the relationship.

Moreover, engaging in personal interests allows for a healthy space apart, which can enhance the relationship's allure. It's the classic case of absence making the heart grow fonder. By spending time apart and engaging in individual pursuits, you give yourselves the chance to miss each other, making the time spent together even more precious.

Finally, it's crucial to remember that investing in personal and shared interests is a continuous process. As you and your partner grow, so will your interests. What's important is keeping the communication lines

grow, so will your interests. What's important is keeping the communication lines open, being receptive to trying new things, and supporting each other's personal growth journeys. This dynamic interplay of individuality and togetherness is what makes a relationship truly healthy and fulfilling.

In summary, the secret sauce to maintaining your identity while nurturing a relationship lies in the delicate balance between personal and shared interests. It's about celebrating and respecting your individuality while embracing the beauty of growth and discovery together. So, dare to explore, engage, and invest in interests both personal and shared. By doing so, you not only enrich your own life but also bring a wealth of experiences, joy, and depth to your relationship.

Remember, a relationship thrives best when both partners are their whole, authentic selves—investing in what makes them uniquely them while finding joy in shared adventures. Embrace this journey with an open heart and mind, and watch as your relationship flourishes amidst love, respect, and mutual growth.

Chapter 17

When Challenges
Arise

In any relationship, encountering challenges is inevitable. It's not a matter of if, but when. How we handle these hurdles can significantly impact the health and longevity of our connections. Accepting this reality is the first step toward navigating relationship challenges with grace and resilience. It's easy to glorify the early stages of romance, where everything feels new and exciting. However, as we move deeper into our relationships, the veneer of perfection fades, revealing the gritty truths of our human imperfections.

Effective communication is paramount during these testing times. It's not just about speaking but also about listening with empathy and understanding. When disagreements arise, it's crucial to address them head-on, rather than letting resentments fester. Misunderstandings, if left unchecked, can snowball into larger issues that are much harder to resolve. Remember, encountering problems doesn't mean your relationship is flawed; it means you're both human. The key lies in tackling these issues together, as a team, rather than letting them drive a wedge between you.

Setting and respecting boundaries is another critical component of navigating challenges. Boundaries aren't constraints meant to limit your partner or yourself; they're a way to respect each other's individuality, preferences, and comfort zones. Sometimes, the biggest challenge in a relationship is recognizing when your boundaries or your partner's are being crossed and addressing this infringement constructively. This requires a delicate balance of assertiveness and sensitivity—a skill that, like any other, gets better with practice.

There will be moments when the challenge at hand seems insurmountable. In these moments, it's essential to reflect on why you chose each other in the first place. Revisiting the foundation of your relationship can be a powerful reminder of your mutual respect, love, and the dreams you have built together. It's also an opportunity to acknowledge how much you've grown, both individually and as a couple. Growth often happens in the face of adversity; it's how diamonds are formed under pressure, after all.

Finally, know when to seek outside support. It's okay to admit that some challenges are beyond what you can handle alone. Whether it's turning to trusted friends, family, or professionals, getting an external perspective can provide clarity and guidance. Understanding that it's not a sign of weakness but a step toward a stronger, healthier relationship is crucial. As you navigate through these trials together, you'll find that your bond deepens, built on a foundation of mutual support, understanding, and an unbreakable commitment to facing life's storms as one.

Chapter 18

Conflict Resolution

Having navigated through the complexities of understanding oneself, entering the dating scene, and establishing a healthy relationship, we find ourselves at a crucial juncture - resolving conflicts. It's an inevitable part of any relationship, a test of its strength and durability. Conflict, when approached with the right mindset, can be an opportunity for growth rather than a stumbling block. It's all about the art of negotiation, empathy, and, most importantly, understanding.

In the realm of conflict resolution, the first step is to approach disagreements with a sense of calm and a willingness to listen. It may seem counterintuitive, but it's crucial to validate your partner's feelings before rushing to find a solution. This doesn't mean you agree with them on every point, but it does mean you acknowledge their emotions are valid. Such validation creates a safe space for open dialogue, mitigating the defensiveness that often escalates arguments.

Once both partners feel heard and understood, it's time to collaboratively work towards a resolution. This is where compromise comes into play. Compromise doesn't mean both parties lose; rather, it's about finding a solution that both can live with, understanding that maintaining the health of the relationship is more important than winning an argument. Discussing each other's needs and finding common ground can turn a conflict into a stepping stone towards deeper understanding and intimacy.

Importantly, after navigating through a disagreement, it's essential to take time to reflect both individually and as a couple. This reflective process is a crucial component of strengthening the relationship post-conflict. It's about learning from the disagreement, recognizing patterns that may lead to conflict, and brainstorming ways to handle similar situations more constructively in the future. Implementing what you've learned will not only minimize future conflicts but also enhance the quality of your relationship.

Finally, it's significant to remember that conflict resolution skills are honed over time and require patience and consistent practice. Every conflict resolved constructively is a step towards a more stable, fulfilling relationship. It strengthens the bond between partners, fostering resilience against future challenges. Thus, embracing conflict as an inevitable, yet manageable, aspect of your relationship journey is key to building a lasting partnership.

Managing Disagreements

In the realm of relationships, disagreements are as inevitable as the changing seasons. They're a natural part of two unique individuals coming together, each with their own thoughts, beliefs, and feelings. What differentiates a healthy relationship from a struggling one, though, isn't the absence of disagreements, but how they are managed. The goal isn't to avoid disagreement but to navigate them in a way that strengthens the bond between partners.

First and foremost, it's critical to approach disagreements with a mindset geared towards understanding rather than winning. This shift in perspective can transform conflicts from battlegrounds into platforms for insight and deeper connection. Effective communication plays a pivotal role here. It involves actively listening to your partner, acknowledging their feelings and viewpoint, and expressing your own thoughts and emotions clearly and respectfully. By doing so, you create an environment where both partners feel heard and valued, which is the cornerstone of resolving disagreements amicably.

Another important aspect is timing. Not every moment is right for addressing a disagreement. It's essential to choose a time when both partners are calm and prepared to engage in a constructive discussion. Attempting to resolve a conflict in the heat of the moment, when emotions are running high, can lead to words or actions that exacerbate the situation. Patience and timing can greatly increase the likelihood of a positive outcome.

It's also valuable to remember that compromise is not a sign of defeat but a testament to the strength of the relationship. Finding a middle ground where both partners can agree or at least understand the other's stance underpins the art of compromise. This doesn't mean sacrificing your own needs or values but rather finding solutions that respect both partners' perspectives. A willingness to compromise can significantly diminish the intensity and duration of disagreements.

Lastly, reflecting on disagreements after they've been resolved is a powerful tool for growth. This reflection isn't about assigning blame but understanding how the disagreement arose, how it was handled, and how similar situations can be better managed in the future. Such reflections can turn conflicts into valuable learning experiences, fostering a culture of continuous improvement in the relationship. With each successfully resolved disagreement, partners can build a stronger, more resilient bond, equipped to handle the challenges that life may throw their way.

Strengthening the Relationship Post-Conflict

After navigating through a disagreement or a conflict, it's natural to experience a myriad of emotions, from relief to residual hurt. However, this period also presents a golden opportunity to fortify your relationship, transforming potential weaknesses into strengths. Open, vulnerable discussions about feelings and thoughts that arose during the conflict can lead to deeper understanding and empathy between partners. Remember, it's not just about moving past a fight; it's about growing together from the experience.

Rebuilding trust plays a crucial role in this recovery phase. This involves not just verbal affirmations but consistent actions that reinforce your commitment to each other and to the relationship's wellbeing. Establishing new agreements or adjusting existing ones can be part of this phase, allowing both partners to feel heard and their needs respected. Keep in mind, these agreements are living documents of your relationship, meant to evolve as you both grow.

Emotional connection and intimacy often need a reboot after conflicts. Integrating enjoyable shared activities or rituals can aid in healing and reconnection. Whether it's a weekly date night, a shared hobby, or simply a few moments of quiet coffee time in the morning, these practices can serve as reminders of the joy and love that exists between you. It's about creating positive memories to balance out the challenging ones.

Communication, as always, is the cornerstone of not just resolving conflicts but in preventing many from happening in the first place. Post-conflict, it might be helpful to gently revisit the discussion about what led to the disagreement, with a focus on understanding each other's perspectives rather than assigning blame. This could also be a time to explore and possibly improve your communication styles, ensuring you're both equipped with the skills to express yourselves clearly and respectfully.

Finally, acknowledging and celebrating the fact that you've navigated through a conflict together is crucial. Overcoming challenges as a team can strengthen your bond, instilling confidence in the relationship's durability. Each conflict overcome is a testament to your commitment to each other and the relationship. With empathy, understanding, and a willingness to grow together, you can turn post-conflict periods into powerful moments of strengthening your bond.

Chapter 19

Seeking

Support

In navigating the complex world of relationships, recognizing when you need support isn't just a sign of strength—it's a crucial step toward building a healthier, happier partnership. It's easy to fall into the trap of believing that we should be able to manage everything on our own or that seeking help is a sign of weakness. However, the opposite is true. Admitting you could use some guidance and seeking it out actively highlights your commitment to the health and success of your relationship. Whether it's turning to trusted friends, family, or professionals, understanding when and how to ask for support is key. It's about enriching and strengthening your bond with your partner by acknowledging that sometimes, a little outside perspective can make all the difference.

Utilizing couples therapy is one method of seeking support that can be profoundly effective in overcoming relationship hurdles. It's a space where both parties can express their feelings and thoughts openly, guided by a professional who can provide unbiased feedback and strategies for improvement. Couples therapy isn't just for relationships in crisis; it can be a preventive measure, helping to resolve minor issues before they escalate into significant problems. Moreover, it serves as a tool for personal growth, offering insights into your behavior patterns, communication styles, and emotional responses. Embracing therapy can lead to breakthroughs not just in your relationship, but in your personal development journey as well.

Knowing when to ask for help is just as important as knowing where to find it. This step requires a level of self-awareness and openness that can take time to develop. But when you do decide to reach out, it can transform the dynamics of your relationship for the better. Whether it's identifying when you need professional intervention or simply needing a listening ear, the act of seeking support is a testament to the resilience and depth of your partnership. Embrace it as part of your journey together, and remember, seeking support is not just about navigating the rough patches; it's also about amplifying the joy, connection, and love between you.

Knowing When to Ask for Help

In the grand journey of seeking and nurturing relationships, it becomes inevitable that at some points, the waves might get too high, the boat might rock too hard, and steering through the storm alone isn't just difficult—it's unadvisable. Often, we're led to believe that seeking help is a sign of weakness, but in the tapestry of human connections, it's arguably the bravest thing one can do. Recognizing that you need guidance, support, or simply an external perspective is not only wise but integral to fostering healthy relationships.

As we embark on this exploration, it's essential to understand that our emotional luggage, if not unpacked properly, can lead to repetitive patterns that sabotage our hopes for a fulfilling partnership. If you find yourself constantly hitting the same roadblocks, feeling drained, or if your relationship is in a repetitious cycle of unresolved conflict, it's a signal. A signal that perhaps it's time to reach out for a helping hand.

Communication struggles are another common trigger for seeking external support. When conversations that once flowed effortlessly turn into minefields, or when what used to be small disagreements escalate into full-blown arguments with no resolution in sight, these are not just bumps on the road—they're indications that the relationship could benefit from professional guidance.

The journey towards understanding when to seek help also involves recognizing shifts in your emotional or mental well-being. If your relationship is causing persistent sadness, anxiety, or is impacting your self-esteem and confidence, these are not just personal battles. They're intertwined with your relationship dynamics and addressing them with a professional can provide the tools and insights needed to navigate through these complex emotions.

It's also worth noting that asking for help doesn't necessarily mean that your relationship is failing or that you're not capable of resolving issues on your own. On the contrary, it's a proactive step towards ensuring the health and longevity of your partnership. Seeking therapy, for instance, can be an enriching experience that strengthens the bond between partners by improving communication, deepening understanding, and resolving underlying issues that might be too challenging to tackle alone.

Understanding when to ask for help is a process that requires introspection and honesty with oneself. It involves setting aside ego and acknowledging that like any journey worth embarking on, the path of relationships is sometimes better navigated with a guide. Couples therapy, support groups, or even workshops aimed at enhancing relational skills can serve as valuable resources in this regard.

The decision to seek help should also be a mutual one, approached with openness and without blame. It's an opportunity for both partners to express their needs, fears, and desires within the relationship, facilitating a deeper connection and mutual growth. Framing it as a shared journey towards a healthier partnership can help alleviate any apprehension and foster a supportive environment for change.

Unfortunately, the stigma surrounding therapy and asking for help often dissuades couples from taking this step, leaving them to navigate their issues in isolation. Breaking down these barriers by normalizing the pursuit of professional assistance is crucial. Embracing vulnerability and recognizing that seeking help is an act of courage can transform how we perceive and approach our relationships.

In conclusion, knowing when to ask for help is an instrumental part of nurturing a healthy, resilient relationship. It's about recognizing that some chapters of our journey might require assistance from someone who can provide the tools, knowledge, and perspective needed to move forward. It's an acknowledgment that together, as a unit, facing challenges with support can lead to a deeper, more fulfilling connection. So, when the waves get high, remember, reaching out for a helping hand is not a sign of weakness—it's the hallmark of a strong partnership.

Utilizing Couples Therapy Effectively

Embarking on couples therapy can often feel like a daunting leap for many. It's a step filled with vulnerability, yet it stands as a testament to the commitment both partners have towards building a stronger foundation together. To navigate this journey effectively, it's crucial to approach therapy with openness and readiness for change.

Firstly, selecting the right therapist is paramount. It's essential to find a professional whose approach resonates with both of you, creating a safe space for honest dialogue. Remember, therapy is a collaborative effort; thus, feeling connected and respected by your therapist lays the groundwork for productive sessions.

Setting clear goals can significantly enhance the therapy experience. Before diving in, sit down together and outline what you both wish to achieve. Whether it's improving communication, resolving specific issues, or simply understanding each other in deeper ways, having shared goals can guide your therapy journey and keep you aligned.

One common misconception is that therapy is a quick fix. It's not. It requires patience, commitment, and the willingness to work through discomfort. Change doesn't happen overnight; it's a process that unfolds at its own pace. Embracing this mindset can help mitigate frustration and unrealistic expectations.

Active participation in sessions is another key to effectiveness. Therapy is not a spectator sport. It demands involvement, reflection, and the courage to be vulnerable. Sharing openly and honestly, while also respectfully listening to your partner, fosters a fertile ground for growth and understanding.

Between sessions, applying the insights and strategies learned is essential. Therapy extends beyond the therapist's office. It's about taking those tools and actively working to integrate them into your daily interactions. This real-world application is where significant change takes root.

Moreover, embracing individual growth within the therapy process can profoundly impact the relationship's dynamic. Personal insights and self-improvement efforts benefit not just the individual but the partnership as a whole. It's a journey of becoming not only better partners but better individuals.

Feedback—both giving and receiving—is a cornerstone of effective therapy. Openly discussing what works and what doesn't within the therapy setting can refine the process, making each session more impactful. Your therapist can adjust techniques and approaches based on this feedback, optimizing the therapeutic experience.

Finally, celebrating progress, no matter how small, reinforces positive change. Acknowledgment of efforts and achievements, both individually and as a couple, fuels motivation and deepens the connection. It serves as a reminder of why you embarked on this journey together, highlighting the value of your partnership and the growth you've achieved.

In conclusion, couples therapy is a powerful tool for strengthening relationships, but its success hinges on both partners' commitment to the process. With the right approach, mindset, and actions both within and outside of therapy, couples can navigate their challenges more effectively, paving the way for a healthier, more resilient partnership.

Chapter 20

Self-Reflection and Assessment

As we've navigated through the complexities of understanding ourselves and stepping into the world of dating with a renewed sense of self, it's imperative to pause and engage in self-reflection and assessment. This phase isn't about critiquing ourselves harshly but about gently acknowledging where we are on our journey and recognizing our growth. It's a moment to ask ourselves, "How have I changed since beginning this journey?" and "What have I learned about my needs and desires?" This intentional pause allows us to align our actions and decisions with our core values and aspirations.

Periodic check-ins with ourselves are not just beneficial; they're essential. Like any meaningful endeavor, our journey toward love and healthy relationships benefits from moments of introspection. These check-ins can take various forms—journaling, meditation, or conversations with trusted friends or mentors. The key here is honesty and openness with oneself. It's about identifying areas of growth as well as areas that still require attention and effort. This ongoing dialogue with oneself fortifies our emotional resilience and enhances our ability to engage in relationships that are nurturing and fulfilling.

Assessing the health of our relationships is equally critical. It involves looking at the dynamics of our interactions and evaluating whether they align with the characteristics of a healthy partnership we've previously outlined. Questions like, "Do I feel respected and valued?" and "Are my boundaries being honored?" help us gauge the quality of our relationships. It's also crucial to recognize how we contribute to the relationship's health, acknowledging both our strengths and areas where we can improve. This balanced assessment fosters an environment of mutual growth and respect.

Embracing the journey toward love requires patience and perseverance. It's a process that doesn't have a definitive endpoint; rather, it's an ongoing evolution of understanding, experiencing, and growing. As we move forward, let's remember to celebrate the progress we've made, no matter how small it might seem. Each step forward is a testament to our commitment to creating and maintaining stable, fulfilling relationships. It's about honoring the person we've become through this process and anticipating the continued growth that lies ahead.

Ultimately, self-reflection and assessment are about embracing the entirety of our journey—its challenges and triumphs. By fostering a deep, compassionate understanding of ourselves and our relationships, we lay the foundation for love that is not only fulfilling but transformative. As we continue to navigate the complexities of relationships, let these moments of introspection be our guiding light, steering us toward connections that enrich our lives and nurture our spirits.

Periodic Check-ins with Yourself

As we journey through the process of self-discovery and toward building meaningful relationships, it's vital to pause and reflect on our own growth and state of being. Periodic check-ins with yourself serve as an essential mechanism for self-assessment and personal reflection. These moments of introspection enable us to understand our feelings, recognize our achievements, and identify areas where we may need further growth or support. Think of these check-ins as routine maintenance for your mental and emotional well-being, ensuring that you stay aligned with your goals and values.

Initiating a check-in with yourself may seem daunting or even unnecessary amid a busy life. However, setting aside time for this practice can profoundly impact your emotional health. Start small, perhaps with a few minutes each week to ask yourself how you're feeling, what's bringing you joy, and what's causing stress or discomfort. You might find it helpful to journal these reflections, giving you a tangible record of your emotional journey and progress over time. This practice fosters a deeper connection with yourself, promoting self-awareness and emotional intelligence—key components in building healthy relationships.

One of the core aspects of these check-ins is to acknowledge and celebrate your growth. Each step forward, no matter how small, is a victory in your journey of self-improvement. Did you handle a stressful situation more calmly than before? Have you made progress in communicating your needs more effectively? Acknowledging these milestones builds self-esteem and resilience, reinforcing your capacity to navigate challenges in both personal and relational contexts.

At the same time, these check-ins allow you to identify and address any negative patterns or behaviors that may emerge. For instance, you might notice a tendency to withdraw emotionally when feeling overwhelmed, or perhaps a pattern of prioritizing others' needs over your own. Recognizing these patterns is the first step toward change. It empowers you to make conscious decisions to break cycles that may hinder your emotional well-being and the health of your relationships.

Finally, periodic check-ins serve as a reminder that growth and self-discovery are ongoing processes. They encourage a mindset of continuous learning and adaptation, essential for navigating the complexities of relationships. By regularly taking stock of your emotional state, celebrating your progress, and addressing challenges, you solidify your foundation of self-awareness and self-care. This foundation not only enriches your personal life but also enhances your ability to engage in healthy, fulfilling relationships with others.

Assessing the Health of the Relationship

Once we've set sail on the vast ocean of love and relationship-building, it's crucial to occasionally drop anchor and evaluate where we are. Think of this as a form of maintenance for your relationship; after all, we wouldn't expect a garden to flourish without regular care and attention. The process of assessing the health of your relationship isn't about nitpicking every minor issue but rather taking a broad and honest look at the foundational elements that keep the partnership strong and vibrant. Are communication lines open and honest? Is there mutual respect and understanding? These questions can serve as a starting point for this vital self-reflective process.

It's not uncommon for couples to shy away from such assessment due to fear of what they might find. However, embracing this step with courage and openness can lead to transformative growth and deepening of the bond. If you discover areas that need improvement, view them as opportunities rather than shortcomings. This approach not only nurtures a healthier relationship but also bolsters individual personal growth. Improvement in communication, for instance, enhances not just your romantic relationships but all aspects of your social life. Remember, identifying and working on weak spots is a sign of commitment and strength, not failure.

Moreover, this evaluating phase shouldn't be a solo task. Engaging your partner in this journey fosters a deeper connection and ensures that both voices are heard. Making this a regular practice, say quarterly or during significant milestones, can help keep the relationship on track and aligned with mutual goals and values. Like sailors navigating the seas with stars, use these assessments as your guideposts. They are an indispensable tool for ensuring that both of you are contributing to a relationship that's not just surviving but thriving.

Embracing the Journey Toward Love

As we navigate through the layers of self-reflection and assessment, it's crucial to remember that the path toward love is as enriching as the destination itself. Embarking on this journey requires patience and a willingness to explore the depths of our own hearts and minds. It's about understanding the value of every step we take, whether we're learning about our emotional needs, exploring our past patterns, or setting boundaries for future relationships. This journey necessitates a blend of courage and vulnerability as we confront and embrace our true selves.

At times, the quest for love may seem daunting, fraught with challenges and unexpected turns. It's natural to encounter moments of doubt or fear. Yet, it's in these very moments that we discover our resilience and capacity for growth. By embracing these experiences, we cultivate a sense of compassion for ourselves and a deep understanding of what it means to love and be loved. This introspective process is not just about finding someone to share our lives with; it's about building a foundation of self-love and self-respect that enriches all aspects of our lives.

Throughout this journey, it's vital to engage in periodic check-ins with ourselves, assessing not only the health of our romantic relationships but also our personal well-being. Reflecting on our progress and the lessons we've learned allows us to adapt and move forward with greater self-awareness. It's a process that encourages us not to rush but to savor each moment, recognizing that every experience, whether joyful or challenging, contributes to our growth.

Fostering a healthy relationship is an ongoing endeavor that extends far beyond the initial stages of dating. It involves continuous communication, mutual respect, and a shared commitment to nurturing the bond. As we strive to maintain the balance between our individual identities and our role within a partnership, we discover the true essence of a loving, supportive relationship. It's about enhancing each other's lives, offering a steadfast foundation of support, and celebrating the journey together.

Ultimately, embracing the journey toward love is about recognizing that this path is as unique as we are. It's a deeply personal experience that shapes our understanding of love, intimacy, and partnership. By remaining open to learning and growing, both individually and within our relationships, we unlock the potential for profound, enduring connections. This journey, with all its twists and turns, is not just about finding love—it's about discovering a deeper connection with ourselves and the world around us.

Appendix A

Mental Health

Resources

Embarking on your journey to discover love while fostering a strong, healthy foundation for yourself and your future relationships is a commendable and empowering path. It's also a journey that, at times, might require support beyond what this book or your immediate circle can offer. Knowing when to seek outside help and having access to the right resources can make all the difference in navigating toward a brighter, healthier future.

Below, we've compiled a list of mental health resources designed to support you wherever you might find yourself on your journey. Whether you're seeking professional advice, looking for community support, or simply need a listening ear, these resources can provide the assistance you need.

National Hotlines and Websites

- **National Suicide Prevention Lifeline:** Available 24/7, this hotline provides free and confidential support for people in distress, prevention and crisis resources.

  Call 1-800-273-TALK (1-800-273-8255).

- **Crisis Text Line:** For those who prefer texting to talking, this service connects you with a trained Crisis Counselor. Text *"HELLO" to 741741.*

- **NAMI (National Alliance on Mental Illness):** This organization offers resources and support for individuals with mental illness and their families. *Visit nami.org* or call 1-800-950-NAMI (1-800-950-6264).

Online Therapy Platforms

- *Talkspace* - This platform connects users with licensed therapists for video, audio, and text therapy sessions.

- *BetterHelp* - Offering a wide range of therapists with various specialties, BetterHelp allows for flexible communication methods.

Support Groups and Community Forums

Connecting with others who understand your experience can be incredibly validating and helpful. Websites such as *Psych Central Forums* and *Mental Health America* offer online communities where individuals can share their stories, challenges, and triumphs. Local community centers and hospitals often have information on in-person support groups as well.

Self-Help and Education

1. Mindfulness and meditation apps like *Headspace* and *Calm* offer guided sessions that can help ease anxiety and improve your overall mental well-being.

2. Books on self-care, emotional resilience, and healthy relationships provide knowledge and coping strategies. Your local library or bookstore can recommend titles relevant to your journey.

Remember, it's okay to ask for help, and it's an act of courage to take steps toward improving your mental health. Utilizing these resources can provide support and guidance as you continue on your path to love and mental wellness. Your journey is unique, and it's okay to seek out the tools and support best suited to your needs and experiences.